Word Whiz's
Guide to
Texas
Middle School
Vocabulary

By Chris Kensler

A Paper Airplane Project

Simon & Schuster
New York ● London ● Sydney ● Singapore ● Toronto

Kaplan Publishing
Published by Simon & Schuster, Inc.
1230 Avenue of the Americas
New York, NY 10020

For bulk sales to schools, colleges, and universities, please contact: Order Department,
Simon & Schuster, 100 Front Street, Riverside, NJ 08075. Phone: 1-800-223-2336. Fax:
1-800-943-9831.

Kaplan® is a registered trademark of Kaplan, Inc.

Cover Design: Cheung Tai
Interior Page Design and Production: Paper Airplane Projects

Manufactured in the United States of America

September 2001

10 9 8 7 6 5 4 3 2 1

Library of Congress Cataloging-in-Publication Data

ISBN 0-7432-1106-5

All of the practice questions in this book were created by the authors to illustrate question types. They are not actual test questions.

Table of Contents

Introduction **5**

English Language Arts
WhizWords **8**
Exercises **17**

Social Studies
WhizWords **20**
Exercises **41**

Math
WhizWords **46**
Exercises **54**

Science
WhizWords **58**
Exercises **72**

Test Instructions
WhizWords **80**
Exercises **84**

All-Purpose Words
WhizWords **86**
Exercises **88**

Answer Pages **90**

About the Author

Chris Kensler grew up in Indiana and attended Indiana University, where he majored in English. He has edited several test-prep publications, worked as feature writer/reporter for a daytime drama publication, and written a book or two, including *Study Smart Junior*, which received the Parents' Choice Award. Currently, he is the editor of an art magazine, is married to the lovely woman who designed this book, and has some cool cats and a dog named Joe.

Sam Antonio is a figment of his imagination.

Acknowledgments

The author would like to thank Maureen McMahon, Lori DeGeorge, and Beth Grupper for their help in shaping and editing the manuscript, and Chris Dreyer for copyediting this book.

The publisher wishes to thank Ryan Blanchette for his contributions to this book.

Introduction

Hi. My name is Sam. Sam Antonio. As you

can probably tell from my name, I'm from Texas. I'm going to help you with your vocabulary.

I'm in the eighth grade. At my school I'm famous for two things—my fastball and my vocabulary. I perfected my fastball last summer by throwing at a 2 foot x 2 foot box every day. Man, my arm felt like a rubber band at first, but now it is strong and my fastball is up to 60 mph—not bad for an eighth grader.

I perfected my vocabulary by practicing, too. By reading books, writing essays and stories, and by just generally paying attention to words. It turned me into a Word Whiz. Now I'm going to turn you into one.

If you're having trouble on tests, one reason might be because you are having trouble understanding the words. Of course, the first and most likely reason you blank or panic or freak out on tests is that instead of studying, you keep watching your new *Chicken Run* DVD. Still, sometimes things don't go so well even when you do study. That's the worst. You're like—I studied all night and I still got a D! What's up with that?

Sometimes it's because you just aren't comfortable with the words on the test. For example, say you are taking a math test and one of the questions asks you to find the "perimeter of a rectangle." It's not hard to do— you just add up all the sides. But if you space out on what the word "perimeter" means, you're in trouble. Your brain freezes. Does it have something to do with periscopes? Or maybe something to do with meters? The next thing you know, you have a picture of a submarine doing the 40-meter dash in your head.

Believe me, I've been there. It's no fun. But it doesn't have to be that way.

Word Whiz Is Here to Help

Believe it or not, you probably already know more than 10,000 words total. It just happens. The older you get, the more words get added to your vocabulary. But let's not talk about the words you already know, let's focus on the words you need to know. The 600-plus words in this book are the most important ones to know for middle school homework, tests, and the TAAS (Texas Assessment of Academic Skills). I call them WhizWords. If you know these WhizWords backward and forward, you will be in good shape at school, and you will no doubt become rich and successful when you grow up.

I'm going to review these WhizWords for you by relating them to things you're probably interested in, like TV, movies, sports, music, celebrities, and the stuff kids like us like to do when we're NOT in school. All these things can help you learn these 600-plus words.

I'm also going to explain them to you in words you already know. The problem with a lot of dictionaries is the words they use in the definition are harder than the word they are defining! Or they just repeat the word. Here's an example—the definition of "impartial" from a popular dictionary (I won't name names):

impartial—*adj.* not partial; unprejudiced.

Gee, thanks a lot! Believe me, if I knew what "partial" meant, I could probably figure out impartial. And "unprejudiced?" How many syllables is that? Eleven? Geez. And of course they don't give a sample sentence. Now here's my definition:

impartial—*adj.* fair. Judges and juries are supposed to be <u>impartial</u>. That means they just go by the facts. Like Judge Judy on TV —she is an <u>impartial</u> judge who listens to all the facts, then she reams the person who is guilty.

Better, right? I'm also only going to give you the one or two meanings that you are most likely to see on a test in class. Some words have tons of different meanings, and regular dictionaries have to list them all. But in my book, I am just going to focus on the meanings that apply to your tests, classroom reading, and homework.

How to Use This Book

Most dictionaries just list all words in alphabetical order. That's a good idea, of course. But I have gone one step further. My WhizWords are in alphabetical order, but I have also divided them into six categories:

English Language Arts   **Science**
Social Studies   **Test Instructions**
Math   **All-Purpose Words**

This way, you can focus on the subjects where you want to improve your vocabulary. Notice that I also included a list of words that you'll probably come across when you're taking the TAAS or other tests, and another list of general words that you'll find useful in all your classes.

Now, each of these chapters has two parts—the vocabulary list, plus some practice exercises. The exercises will help you remember important words that are related to each other. Off to the side of the exercises, you'll see a bunch of icons. These tell you what resources you'll use to do the exercise—things like TV, newspapers, and the Internet. These are the icons:

Life   **School**   **Movie**   **Sports**   **Magazine**

History   **Imagination**   **News**   **Internet**   **Television**

These exercises are like dessert. The main course of the book is my WhizWord lists. The lists give you easy-to-understand definitions and sample sentences like the one I gave you for "impartial." You'll also find all this extra cool stuff:

 My helpful hints on how to learn words and ace tests.

 Really short quizzes to help cement the words in your brain.

 Good stuff to know that is related to a WhizWord.

DOUBLE MEANING WhizWords that can mean two different things.

 Words that mean the same thing as a WhizWord.

 Words that mean the opposite of a WhizWord.

Related Word An important word related to a WhizWord.

On the TAAS How WhizWords are likely to appear on the TAAS.

Okay then. I think I'm done explaining. Have fun, and remember, if you learn all these words, your vocabulary will be really, really good and you should do better on your tests.

Sam Antonio

Chapter 1
English Language Arts

Use an adjective or adverb to describe each of these words:
chewy
green
school
shopping
sports
questions

adjective—*n.* a word that describes a noun or a pronoun. You need to be able to pick out <u>adjectives</u> in sentences, and you also need to use them when you do your own writing. *Bad, good, stupid, smart, rich,* and *poor* are all adjectives.

adverb—*n.* a word that describes a verb, an adjective, or another adverb. What I just said for adjectives goes for <u>adverbs</u>. You can remember what words <u>adverbs</u> modify because all the parts of speech it modifies are part of its name: <u>ad-</u> (adjectives, adverbs) and <u>verb</u> (verbs). *Very, really, not, incredibly, amazingly,* and *obviously* are all <u>adverbs</u>.

analogy—*n.* a way to compare things that are otherwise not similar. For example, to explain how good the Texas Rangers are compared to last year, I might use the <u>analogy</u> of a baby learning to walk: The Texas Rangers were like a newborn baby a few years ago, they couldn't do anything! But now, with Alex Rodriguez, they have learned to walk—and even run!

Related Word

**analysis—n.
close study.**

analyze—*v.* to study carefully to figure out something. I must say, after <u>analyzing</u> all the latest Internet search engines, I still like Yahoo! the best. It is fast, gets me the best results, and is easiest to navigate.

antonym—*n.* the opposite word. *Good* is the <u>antonym</u> of *bad. Over* is the <u>antonym</u> of *under.* I have listed <u>antonyms</u> for lots of words throughout this book.

biography—*n.* a book about someone's life. An autobiography is a <u>biography</u> written by the person it is about. The new <u>biography</u> of Jennifer Lopez that my big sister Pam bought was the worst book I have ever read. Period.

characteristics—*n.* special qualities. In English Language Arts, physical <u>characteristics</u> usually describe a character in a story or the story's setting. For example, some <u>characteristics</u> of Frankenstein include a high, square forehead and rivets coming out of the sides of his head.

To remember characteristics, think of the word "character"—characters have characteristics.

chronological—*adj.* in the order events happened. Tests are always asking you to put events in <u>chronological</u> order, or to be able to take a set of <u>chronological</u> events and write a story about them.

Jim Carrey's best movies, in <u>chronological</u> order, are *Ace Ventura: Pet Detective* (1994), *Ace Ventura: When Nature Calls* (1995), *Liar Liar* (1997), and *How the Grinch Stole Christmas* (2000).

clarify—*v.* to make clearer. On tests, you will often be asked to <u>clarify</u> sentences and what characters in stories are talking about. For example: "Jim Carrey's comedic brilliance over the span of his film career is unsurpassed in the history of cinema" can be <u>clarified</u> as "Jim Carrey is funnier than anyone, ever."

cliché—*n.* a saying that is used too much. For example, it is a <u>cliché</u> to call cafeteria food dog food, because so many people have called it dog food before. In general, when writing a story, you want to avoid using <u>clichés</u>.

coherent—*adj.* making sense. It is important that sentences and paragraphs have a <u>coherent</u> structure. If you are telling a story, the first thing comes first, the second thing comes second, and so on. It is also important for people to be <u>coherent</u>. Newscasters, for instance, have to be <u>coherent</u> so we can understand what they're saying.

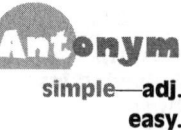

Antonym
incoherent—adj.
confused.

compare—*v.* to find the similarities in two or more things. (See the definition of *contrast*.)

complex—*adj.* complicated, made up of a bunch of connected parts. On lots of tests you are asked to read <u>complex</u> passages and find the important information in them. It's like watching a murder mystery on TV and trying to figure out who did it. The mystery is <u>complex</u>, but if you pay attention and concentrate, you can figure out who the culprit is.

Antonym
simple—adj.
easy.

compound—*adj.* in English Language Arts, a word made of two or more other words is a compound word. *Carpetbagger* (carpet + bagger) is a <u>compound</u> word. (See Social Studies for the definition of *carpetbagger*.) <u>Compound</u> sentences are two sentences connected with a conjunction or a comma. *Example*: I really like her, but I am afraid to talk to her.

concise—*adj.* short and to the point. When you are writing, try to be <u>concise</u>. Judge Judy on TV is very concise in her rulings. She usually says something like "You're wrong, you're an idiot,

English Language Arts

On the TAAS

Based on the information given, what conclusion could you arrive at?

you're guilty!" Now that's <u>concise</u>.

conclusion—*n.* judgment or decision. Many tests ask you what <u>conclusion</u> you can draw from a passage or what <u>conclusion</u> someone in a story came to. That just means you need to be able to sum up what you read. For example, after I read the box score from the last Texas Rangers game, I came to the <u>conclusion</u> that they need a few more good hitters. Only three guys on the team are hitting over .300.

conflict—*n.* a clash of ideas; a clash of characters. Most good writing centers around <u>conflict</u>—two people who can't stand each other, or two ideas that are really different. For example, I am writing a screenplay called *Pretty Dumb* about two actresses who can't stand each other. There is a lot of <u>conflict</u> between the two.

conjunction—*n.* a word that joins words or groups of words in a sentence. There are only a handful of them. The most common are: *and, or, for, but, yet.*

Use all these conjunctions in one looooooong sentence. Come on, it'll be fun! Here, I'll do it first: I ate a peanut butter and jelly sandwich, but I was still hungry, for I hadn't eaten breakfast, so I looked for a cookie, either chocolate chip or oatmeal would do, yet I had a craving for a Rice Krispies Treat. (You can see why run-on sentences are not a good idea.)

contemporary—*adj.* of this time. In English Language Arts, the word is usually used when talking about <u>contemporary</u> writers, which means writers who are writing stuff now. R. L. Stine is a contemporary writer. So is J. K. Rowling.

context—*n.* the setting a word or statement appears in. It's important to know <u>context</u> when you are trying to figure out what someone means. If someone yells "Stop!" the <u>context</u> of that yell tells you why he is yelling. Is he stealing a car? Or is he going to drive off a cliff? Or both? If you know the <u>context</u>, you can answer the question.

contraction—*n.* the shortened form of two words. Haven't = have + not. It's = it + is.

contrast—*v.* to find the differences. This word is most often used in test questions that ask you to "compare and <u>contrast</u>." That just means write about the similarities AND the differences. Like: Compare and <u>contrast</u> supermodel/actress James King and actress/pin-up star Pamela Anderson.

Turn the following into their contractions:
is + not
we + are
were + not
she + is

credible—*adj.* believable. In a trial, a <u>credible</u> witness is a witness the jury can believe. On a test, a <u>credible</u> answer is one that you think could be true. So if I said Pamela Anderson and James King were both the best actresses in the world, that's not really a <u>credible</u> statement. If I said both are blonde and beautiful—that's <u>credible</u>.

WhizTip

To remember credible means "believable," think of incredible, which means "really hard to believe."

critical—*adj.* finding fault. As in <u>critical reading</u>, it means reading a story so you can pick it apart later. <u>Critical reading</u> is kind of the opposite of reading for fun. When you are reading <u>critically</u>, you are reading a story so you can answer questions about it. Usually this means circling, underlining, and making notes as you go along.

culture—*n.* all of the artistic, scientific, and social accomplishments of a group of people. Basically everything a group of people does makes up that society's <u>culture</u>. Traditionally, American <u>culture</u> has been summed up as "baseball, hot dogs, and apple pie." I'll agree with the baseball part, but I'm not sure about the other two.

dialect—*n*. how a particular part of a country speaks. Where you come from is usually where you get your <u>dialect</u>. There is a soft Southern <u>dialect</u>, a hard, grating East Coast <u>dialect</u>—and of course our famous twangy Texan <u>dialect</u>! Authors use <u>dialect</u> in stories to give readers information about character and setting.

dialogue—*n*. the spoken conversations written in a book or a play, usually in quotation marks. Here's some dialogue from *Pretty Dumb*, the screenplay I'm writing for supermodel James King and actress Pamela Anderson. "Oh Pam—my blonde hair is a mess. Poor me. What brand of conditioner do you use?" asked James. "I use Fanteen Selectives, with blonde highlights," Pamela replied, "but you can't borrow it."

euphemism—*n*. the act of substituting an inoffensive word or phrase for an offensive one. For example, "passed away" is a <u>euphemism</u> for "died." "We are in a rebuilding year" is a <u>euphemism</u> in sports for "We are terrible this year, please be patient."

evaluate—*v*. to consider. Tests ask you to <u>evaluate</u> information all of the time. That just means you need to read everything they give you and consider the information before making a decision on an answer. My mom often <u>evaluates</u> the food she is buying at the grocery store by looking at the ingredients to see how much fat is in it. She hates fat.

evidence—*n*. clues and facts. Part of the fun of watching detective shows is following the detective as he uncovers <u>evidence</u> and trying to figure out "whodunnit" before he does. I especially like reruns of *Columbo*—you know, that short dude in the trenchcoat.

figurative language—*n*. the use of metaphors. Instead of writing "Emmitt Smith is a great football player," a sports reporter using <u>figurative language</u> would write "Emmitt Smith is a football player as great as the Rocky Mountains are tall." (See the definition for *metaphor* for more on this.)

flashback—*n*. a point in a story where the narrative goes back in time for a little while before continuing forward. Books and movies use <u>flashbacks</u> all the time, usually to give you more information about a character or the plot. Sometimes in movies and on TV, they signal a <u>flashback</u> by making the screen get all wiggly or fuzzy.

foreshadow—*v*. to hint at what is to come later in a story. A writer may <u>foreshadow</u> that two young characters are going to get married later in the book by having each of them, separately, talk to people about how much they want to get married when they get older.

genre—*n*. a type of writing. Romance, horror, mystery, and sci-fi are all fiction <u>genres</u>. My favorite <u>genre</u> is horror, especially R. L.

DOUBLE MEANING
culture—n. the growth of cells in a laboratory in a petri dish (science).

Whiz Quiz

List three euphemisms you or your parents use:

1. _____

2. _____

3. _____

Whiz Tip

Remember flashback by thinking of the word "back."

Whiz Tip

Remember foreshadow by thinking of the word "forward."

- Stine horror.

- **homonym**—*n.* one of two words that are spelled alike and sound alike but mean different things. *Lie* (to tell an untruth) and *lie* (to rest) are <u>homonyms</u>.

- **identify**—*v.* to pick out. English tests often ask you to <u>identify</u> the protagonist or to <u>identify</u> the verb or to <u>identify</u> the simile.

- **idiom**—*n.* word or phrase that means something it doesn't really mean. Confused? Here are a few <u>idioms</u>:
    - *ants in your pants* means *you are fidgety*
    - *born with a silver spoon in your mouth* means *your parents are rich*
    - *stop bugging me* means *stop bothering me*

- **imagery**—*n.* mental pictures; using figurative language to create scenes and moods. Writers use <u>imagery</u> to make their stories more interesting. Here's an example from my screenplay, with the imagery underlined: Pamela Anderson rose from bed and <u>stretched like a baby bird breaking from its egg</u>. She had a hard day ahead. She and James King were up for the same part in the new Jim Carrey movie. Whoever got the part would be the toast of the town. Whoever lost would feel <u>lower than the dirt on the soles of their six-inch stiletto heels</u>. The movie's producer, Fabio, would make his decision today.

- **infer**—*v.* to conclude. Tests always ask what you can "infer" from the information given. That means you need to figure things out, even if they aren't stated in black and white. For example, you can <u>infer</u> in my screenplay that James King isn't very quick, because whenever anyone asks her a question, she replies, "Huh, what?" Either that or she's hard of hearing.

- **interpersonal**—*adj.* between two people. The <u>interpersonal</u> relationship between James King and Pamela Anderson is very important to my screenplay. At the beginning, they are the best of friends, but as the pressure to get the female lead in the new Jim Carrey movie intensifies, they start to hate each other with a burning passion.

- **interpret**—*v.* to explain. <u>Interpreting</u> is a lot like inferring (see the definition for *infer*)—it means you consider the information you have and try to figure out what it means.

- **interview**—*n.* a conversation in which one person asks the questions and the other answers. One great way to learn about lots of different people is to read <u>interviews</u> in magazines. <u>Interviews</u> can be easier to read than novels and short stories. You can usually read one front-to-back in 30 minutes or less.

- **irony**—*n.* the use of words that mean the opposite of what you mean. A good example is when you say "Gee, I can't wait to go to the dentist and get those cavities filled" in a sarcastic tone, when going to the dentist is obviously the last thing you want to do.

literal—*adj.* the real, dictionary meaning. What a word or phrase or any kind of writing or speaking actually means. "Go jump in a lake" usually doesn't mean someone wants you to get wet. But the <u>literal</u> meaning of the phrase is exactly that—go take a leap into the nearest pond, buddy.

metaphor—*n.* figurative use of words in which a word or phrase is used to mean something other than what it usually means. As you can probably tell by now, English Language Arts is all about using words in creative ways, just like the fine arts are about using paint and clay in creative ways. For a creative writer, <u>metaphors</u> are as important as paint is for an artist. In my screenplay *Pretty Dumb*, I use metaphors all the time. Here are a couple. Fabio was a filmmaking *machine*, churning out two to three movies a year. Pamela's career was in *overdrive*. Every part she wanted, she got. (See also the definition for *simile*—it's a lot *like* <u>metaphor</u>.)

mood—*n.* in English Language Arts, it's the general feeling created by a writer. The <u>mood</u> of a story can be sad or happy or dark or light. The writer creates the <u>mood</u> of a story by using *imagery*, *metaphors,* and all of the other writing tools. By reading a story carefully, you should be able to get a sense of its <u>mood</u>.

motivation—*n.* in English Language Arts, it is the reason a character does something. Tests often ask you to write down a character's <u>motivation</u>. For example: In my screenplay for *Pretty Dumb*, James King ended up talking about Pamela Anderson behind her back. What was James's <u>motivation</u>? You look for the part of the story that made James trash Pamela.

myth—*n.* a story about gods and heroes. My favorite <u>myth</u> is about the snake-haired Medusa: If you look right at her, you turn into Stone Phillips! Or do you just turn to stone . . . I can't remember.

paraphrase—*v.* to express something using different words. Tests often ask you to <u>paraphrase</u> a story or a character's views. That just means write down what happened in the story or what a character thinks in a few sentences. I have to be able to <u>para-phrase</u> my screenplay *Pretty Dumb* in just a few words when I go try to sell it to Hollywood. Here it goes: Three days, two blonde actresses, one juicy movie role.

parody—*n.* a humorous mockery. <u>Parodies</u> mimic "normal" writing genres like horror, mystery, and romance. A good movie example of a <u>parody</u> is *The Pink Panther* series, starring Peter Sellers, from the 1960s and '70s. It is a parody of "normal" detective movies. Watch it—you will laugh and laugh and laugh.

persuade—*v.* to convince. Writers will often try to <u>persuade</u> the readers that their point of view is correct. Tests often ask you to figure out what the writer is trying to <u>persuade</u> you to think. I

English Language Arts

Write down your favorite (or least favorite) platitude:

_____
_____
_____

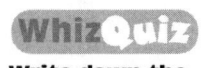

Write down the premise of the last movie you saw:

_____
_____
_____
_____
_____

To remember prophecy, think of the word "prophet." In the Bible, prophets predict what God is going to do.

am persuading you to learn the word persuade. Persuaded?

platitude—*n.* a statement that's a cliché. "The early bird gets the worm" is a platitude. "Slow and steady wins the race" is a platitude.

point of view—*n.* one way of looking at things. A character's point of view is that character's way of thinking. For example, in my screenplay *Pretty Dumb*, it is James King's point of view that Pamela Anderson is too old for the female lead in a Jim Carrey movie. Pamela Anderson's point of view is that James King is a silly supermodel who would turn the Jim Carrey movie into a disaster. Each tries to persuade the movie's producer, Fabio, that her point of view is the correct one.

premise—*n.* the basis for a story. The premise of my screenplay *Pretty Dumb* is two blonde actresses are gunning for the same part, and the person who decides who gets the part, Fabio, is evil.

preposition—*n.* a word that relates a noun or a pronoun to the other words in the sentence. Some popular prepositions are: *by, at, to, with, in, for, from.* What's that spell? BATWIFF. (You swing the bat, you whiff.) Cherish it. Remember it.

preview—*n.* an advance showing. When I go to the movies, my favorite part is the movie previews before the feature presentation. Why? The previews are always good, but the feature presentation is not always good.

progression—*n.* movement forward toward a goal. It is good if your grades show a steady progression upwards. If you are getting lots of Cs, try to start a progression up to Bs, and then to As.

proofread—*v.* to check spelling and grammar. It is important to proofread your papers before you hand them in because good spelling and grammar count toward your grade.

propaganda—the kind of writing that a government or group uses to get you to believe something. Propaganda is used all the time during wars, when one country tells its citizens that the other country is the worst country in the world. And the other country has propaganda that says the same thing about the first country. With propaganda, facts aren't important—it is convincing readers to believe them that is important.

prophecy—*n.* a prediction. Prophecies often have to do with the end of the world and stuff like that. In my screenplay *Pretty Dumb*, Pamela Anderson goes to the fortune teller, who makes a prophecy that Pamela will get a big part in a big movie starring a famous comedian.

relevant—*adj.* pertaining to the matter at hand. Tests often tell you to "consider the relevant information" before choosing your answer. You can remember what "relevant" means by thinking of the word *related.* Relevant information is *related* to the question.

resolution—*n.* the end of a story; how something is resolved. If there is a question about a story's <u>resolution</u>, that means the question is about how it ends. I don't want to give away the <u>resolution</u> of my screenplay *Pretty Dumb*, but let's just say there's some hair pulling and a few stiletto heels get broken . . . .

revise—*v.* to edit; to correct and improve. Sometimes you have to <u>revise</u> a report for class. That means edit it and make it clearer. My mom asked me to <u>revise</u> my screenplay so her favorite singer, Barbra Streisand, could make a cameo appearance.

similarities—*n.* traits that are almost the same; characteristics that are similar. Tests are always asking you about <u>similarities</u> and differences in characters, plots, settings, and stories. Being able to pick out <u>similarities</u> and differences means you understand what you are reading. (See the definitions for *compare* and *contrast* for more on this.)

simile—*n.* a comparison of unlike things that uses the words *like* or *as*. James is crazy <u>like</u> a fox. Pamela is smart <u>as</u> a whip. (By the way—those examples are both also *clichés*.)

speculate—*v.* to think about; to guess at. You are often asked to <u>speculate</u> as to why a character did what he did. That means you need to think about who that character is and why he would do what he did. For example, if you are asked to <u>speculate</u> as to why Fabio stops returning calls from both James King and Pamela Anderson, you would have to look at the actresses' behavior and why Fabio may get sick and tired of talking to them after a while.

summary—*n.* a short recap of the main points of a story. One of the main things you do in English class is <u>summarize</u> what you read. The best way to write a <u>summary</u> is to recap the story in the order things happened, so you don't forget anything.

suspense—*n.* the state of not knowing what will happen, otherwise known as the thing that puts you on the edge of your seat. Writers use <u>suspense</u> all of the time to keep you turning the pages. If you already know what's going to happen, why read on? In my screenplay, I use <u>suspense</u> the whole way—you don't find out which actress gets the part in the Jim Carrey movie until the very end.

symbolism—*n.* the use of a symbol to stand for something real. For example, there are a lot of memorials in Washington, DC, that <u>symbolize</u> the soldiers who lost their lives in our wars. Writers use <u>symbolism</u> when they need to say something without really saying it. An example of this is when a writer <u>symbolizes</u> the passing of seasons by following a leaf as it falls from a tree and then decays on the ground, then feeds the roots of the tree it fell from.

synonym—*n.* a word that means the same thing as another word. *Daring* and *adventurous* are <u>synonyms</u>. *Timid* and *cowardly* are <u>synonyms</u>. When you are writing, instead of using the

Antonym
differences—**n.
things that are,
you guessed it,
different.**

WhizQuiz
**Write a one-
sentence** summary
**of the last book
you read.**
_____
_____
_____
_____

same word over and over, try to use <u>synonyms</u> to change things up a little bit. So if you use the word *car* in the first sentence, use *automobile* in the second and *vehicle* in the third.

tact—*n*. the ability to say something in a way so as not to hurt someone's feelings. A <u>tactful</u> way to tell someone she has bad breath is "Want a breath mint?" not "Hey, your breath stinks." When possible, it is always best to use <u>tact</u>.

timeline—*n*. a graphical representation of a chronology; having a bunch of dates in chronological order on a line. <u>Timelines</u> are all over tests. Sometimes you have to write a story from a <u>timeline</u>. Sometimes you have to read a timeline to see what happened in what order. Here's an example from my screenplay:

Pretty Dumb: Monday

10am—James meets with Fabio	3pm—Pamela goes on *Extra* and trashes James	7pm—James and Pamela get in a fight at the Golden Globes

9am—Pamela meets with Fabio	1pm—Pamela and James have lunch	5pm—James goes on *Access Hollywood* and trashes Pamela	11pm—Fabio has a late-night meeting with a mystery actress

tragedy—*n*. in English Language Arts, a tragedy is a serious play that ends with a very sad ending. Shakespeare wrote the best <u>tragedies</u>, like *Hamlet* and *Macbeth*. My screenplay *Pretty Dumb* is kind of a <u>tragedy</u>: in the end, nobody wins. Neither James nor Pamela gets the part. Fabio gives it to Barbra Streisand instead. James quits the business and becomes a hermit in a windowless shack in Montana. Pamela pays the bills selling chicken roasters on the Home Shopping Network. The End.

verbal—*adj*. having to do with talking and words. The <u>verbal</u> sections of tests are about words, reading, and vocabulary.

verifiable—*adj*. provable; able to be verified. Something that is verifiable is something that can be proved with facts. Your age is <u>verifiable</u>—you just have to show your birth certificate.

WhizWords

analyze
clarify
compare
contrast
evaluate

English Language Arts
Thinking Big

Lots of times when you're taking tests, you're asked to do a math problem or write down a date or name that you have memorized. These kinds of test questions basically test your memory. If you remember what you memorized, you'll be just fine.

But sometimes you have to do a little more than just remember. Sometimes you have to really think about information on the test, and figure out on your own what you think and how you should write it down. These kinds of questions ask you to **analyze** a problem; **evaluate** the situation; **compare** and **contrast** ideas; and **clarify** your answer.

When these words appear in test questions, some kids freeze because they know a lot is expected of them—at least a lot more than just writing down a simple definition for a social studies test or identifying a shape on a geometry test. A good way to stop yourself from freezing is to get used to **analyzing, evaluating, comparing** and **contrasting,** and **clarifying** in situations that aren't so scary.

WhizTip

One great way to build your vocabulary is to hear the words read aloud. So, until they make an audio version of this book, ask an adult to play an audio book you like when you are driving around. Your local library probably has lots of audio books, just like mine. I personally like to listen to the Harry Potter books.

GETTING DEEP EXERCISE

In this exercise you are going to think deep about shallow things that you know a lot about. First, go back to the English Language Arts WhizWords and refresh your memory about what these five words mean. Now pick a movie star, TV star, or entertainer you actually like or know a lot about. I am going to use Britney Spears as my victim, er, subject.

Write your subject at the top of the page. Now write down our five "getting deep" words along the left side of a piece of paper, about five lines apart. Next to each word, write down a topic relating to your victim, er, subject. Then write a short paragraph that answers the "questions" you have written. Here's mine:

Britney Spears

Analyze her album, *Oops . . . I Did It Again.*
Evaluate her singing.
Clarify her relationship with Justin Timberlake.
Compare and contrast Britney Spears and Christina Aguilera.

Once you have done this with one subject, pick another one and do it again. Keep practicing and you'll get really good at this. The more you see and use these words, the more comfortable you get with them, and the better you'll do on your tests.

WhizWords

analogy
dialogue
figurative language
flashback
foreshadow
imagery
irony
metaphor
simile
symbolism

English Language Arts
Writers' Tools

Good writers know how to use all sorts of tools to keep readers' eyes glued to the page (that's a **metaphor**, by the way). Some writers are so good at it, you just can't stop reading. I keep a flashlight under my bed for nights when my parents tell me to turn out my light and go to sleep, but I just can't stop reading. Good writers make writing look easy, so you don't notice all of the tools they are using.

But on tests, it's important to be able to pick out the tools writers use. Lots of reading questions on the TAAS and other tests ask you to identify things like **irony, symbolism,** and **analogies**—basically all of the words that I have listed above on this page. The only way to learn how to find all of these things is to practice finding them in the stories you read every day.

IDENTIFYING A WRITER'S TOOLS EXERCISE

You are going to have to do a little hunting and gathering for this exercise. I want you to go through your house and get on the Internet and find examples of the following types of stories:

> Newspaper—sports story
> Magazine—fashion story
> Internet (print one out)—movie review
> Newspaper—article from the editorial page
> Internet (print one out)—piece of short fiction
> Magazine—celebrity profile
> Newspaper—political story

Gather these up in one place. Now, over the next week, I want you to read one of these stories every day and:

> 1. <u>Underline</u> the writers' tools
> 2. Write the writer's tool in the margin.

There probably won't be enough room in the margins for some of these. If there isn't, you can write down the writer's tools you identify on Post-It Notes and stick them to the story.

English Language Arts
Adverbs and Adjectives

Imagine a world made up of only nouns and verbs. Actors would be . . . just actors. Not terrible actors, not handsome actors, not overpaid actors . . . just actors. Singers would be . . . just singers. Not gorgeous singers or overproduced singers or singers with voices that only a mother could love. Just . . . singers.

Luckily we have adverbs and adjectives, the words that make life special! Alex Rodriguez is the *best* shortstop in the league with a *sweet* swing, *nimble* feet, and *soft* hands. The Texas Rangers are a *vastly improved* team with *incredible* talent and *limitless* potential.

Yes, **adjectives** and **adverbs**, the simple modifiers of verbs, nouns, and other adjectives and adverbs, give writing its spice. So it is very important to use them when you write. It makes your writing more interesting to read, which gets you better grades on your papers and writing tests. All good things, wouldn't you say?

Adjectives and Adverbs for Your Autobiography
goofy
fast
unbelievable
slow
smelly
late
first
early
straight
green
gawky
crazy
fun
laughable
smart
right
heavenly
regrettable

WRITING YOUR AUTOBIOGRAPHY EXERCISE
If you don't believe me, let me prove it. I want you to try to describe your own life without adjectives and adverbs. Then I want you to describe your life WITH adjectives and adverbs—as many as you can possibly think of.

That's right—it's autobiography time. Grab a pencil and paper. Start by filling out this general outline. List three events in each age bracket that you will write about in your own journal or notebook. Stuff like losing your first tooth, learning to swim, moving to a new town, joining the basketball team—events that are memorable and important to you.

Age
0-4
_____

5-8
_____

9-present
_____

Now write two versions of your autobiography: 1) using no adverbs or adjectives; and 2) using as many adverbs and adjectives as you can think of. Underline the adjectives and adverbs in the second version when you are done. I have provided you with a few adjectives and adverbs that you can use if you get stumped.

Chapter 2

Social Studies

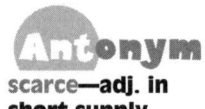

abolish—v. to get rid of.

abolitionist—*n.* someone who fought against slavery. When this country had slavery, there were a bunch of <u>abolitionists</u> trying to free the slaves. Some gave speeches, some ran the underground railroad—all of the <u>abolitionists</u> were working to stop a terrible system.

scarce—adj. in short supply.

abundant—*adj.* plentiful; not scarce. The word is often used to describe natural resources, like <u>abundant</u> coal and oil.

adapt—*v.* to change in response to the surroundings. The word is often used to describe how people and animals <u>adapt</u> as the environment changes. Charles Darwin found that animals <u>adapt</u> to their environments.

adversary—*n.* the enemy! President George W. Bush's <u>adversary</u> in the 2000 presidential election was Al Gore.

Whiz Quiz

Name three rules at school that you advocate:

_____

_____

_____

advocate—*n.* someone who supports a cause. My mom is a big <u>advocate</u> of the new dress code at school because she doesn't have to buy me expensive clothes anymore—just blue pants and a white shirt. If you <u>advocate</u> something, you support it.

aggressor—*n.* the person or country who attacks first. Germany was the <u>aggressor</u> in World War II.

agitator—*n.* someone who stirs things up to bring about change. <u>Agitators</u> are usually described as rebellious and loud-mouthed. Abbie Hoffman was an anti-war <u>agitator</u> during the Vietnam War. He led demonstrations and protests against the war.

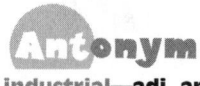

industrial—adj. an economy based on industry (building things).

agrarian—*adj.* pertaining to a culture or economy based on farming and agriculture. The U.S. went from an <u>agrarian</u> economy in the 1800s to an industrial economy in the 1900s. Now there are hardly any farmers left.

allegiance—*n.* a deep commitment to something, like your country or your family. Of course, we have all pledged <u>allegiance</u> to the flag in school.

ally—n. friend; someone in an alliance.

alliance—*n.* an association of people or nations coming together to achieve a common goal. Think of the TV show *Survivor*—the players try to form <u>alliances</u> to protect themselves from getting voted off the show.

ambition—*n.* a burning desire to achieve a goal or to become something. Madonna is often noted for her <u>ambition</u> to become famous. She doesn't have much singing talent, just tons of <u>ambition</u>. The same can be said of lots of actors and politicians.

amendment—*n.* a change to the Constitution. We have had 27 <u>amendments</u> since the Constitution was written in 1789.

Related Word

amend—v. to correct or fix something.

anarchy—*n.* the state of having no government—or anyone else —in charge. <u>Anarchy</u> is usually thought of as a bad thing, with bands of hoodlums running around in the street, breaking windows, and beating people up. Sometimes after a team wins the World Series or the NBA Championship, there is <u>anarchy</u> in the streets when their fans go nuts and start turning over cars and lighting fires.

annex—*v.* to attach or join. You usually hear this word used in situations where a new piece of land is attached to land already owned. Countries <u>annex</u> other countries (usually after they win a war); cities <u>annex</u> surrounding suburbs.

antebellum—*adj.* of the period prior to the Civil War. It's most often used in the phrase "the <u>antebellum</u> South," to describe the South before the Civil War. Think about the movie *Gone With the Wind*: southern gentlemen, women in hoop skirts, plantations— and slaves.

arduous—*adj.* extremely hard or difficult. The word is often used when describing the <u>arduous</u> journey of U.S. settlers west. They could only go a few miles a day in their wagon trains; Native Americans were always attacking them; they got sick and died because there were no doctors; and they didn't even really know what was waiting for them where they were going. Now that's <u>arduous</u>.

WhizQuiz

Write down your three most arduous classes in school:

_____

_____

_____

assert—*v.* to claim; to insist. The colonies <u>asserted</u> their independence from England. They just went and claimed it, no questions asked. During the Civil Rights movement, African Americans <u>asserted</u> their right to vote. In the seventies, feminists asserted their right to equal pay for equal work. As citizens, we assert our rights to do things all the time—no one can stop us. Yes, you could call this country Assertamerica if you wanted!

DOUBLE MEANING
assimilate—v.
when the body
breaks food down
into its nutrients
(science).

assimilate—*v.* to make similar or to absorb into a system or culture. This word is often used when discussing how immigrants are absorbed into American culture. Assimilation is a complex process. Immigrants come here with their own customs. They want to keep some customs, but they also need to adopt some American customs. So the country assimilates them, but it is never easy.

One way to remember **benevolent** is to imagine a nice person named Ben: like Ben Franklin or Ben Affleck.

benevolent—*adj.* kind; caring. Most often used when talking about a "benevolent dictator," which means the dictator has total power, but he uses it for good, not evil. Superman would be a benevolent dictator.

bias—*n.* prejudice. It usually means thinking someone is less than you are for a reason that doesn't make any sense, like gender and skin color. That is bias, or prejudice.

boom and bust economy—*n.* a kind of economy where things go incredibly well for a while, then crash and go incredibly poorly from there on out. It is most often used to describe the California gold rush in the 1800s, where everyone flocked to California for the boom, but once everyone was there and all of the gold had been mined, it all went bust.

boycott—*v.* to refuse to have dealings with a company or country because you disagree with something it does. It is a peaceful way to protest. Instead of picketing or doing something violent, people can boycott. Martin Luther King Jr. convinced black people to boycott the Montgomery, Alabama bus system to protest segregation on the buses. That meant no black people would ride the buses, which meant the buses lost a lot of money. So then they had to pay attention to what Martin Luther King said, or they would go out of business.

buffalo soldiers—*n.* black soldiers who fought against the Native Americans during westward expansion. The Native Americans gave them the name buffalo soldiers because of the courage they displayed in battle.

DOUBLE MEANING
capital—n. the
city where a
state or nation's
government is
located.

capital—*n.* in economics, it means the wealth used to create more wealth. Basically, capital is money or property. If you were going to start a dot-com company, you would need some capital to start with—that includes money to pay your staff, a place to work, and some computers to work on.

capitalist—*n.* in economics, it is the person who owns the wealth used to create more wealth. Donald Trump is a famous capitalist.

capitalize—*v.* to take advantage. My favorite baseball player Alex Rodriguez capitalized on his record as an All-Star shortstop to negotiate a $252 million contract with the Texas Rangers.

carpetbagger—*n.* a politician who runs for office in a state she is not from. Most recently, Hillary Rodham Clinton was called a <u>carpetbagger</u> when she ran for elected office in New York, even though she was not from New York and had never lived there before, either.

censorship—*n.* restriction on what someone can say or do. Although the First Amendment to the Constitution protects our right to freedom of speech, television shows are <u>censored</u>, movies are <u>censored</u>, and songs are <u>censored</u>. <u>Censorship</u> happens every day in this country—usually to protect young people from adult language and situations. Many artists and performers are frustrated by <u>censorship</u> in the United States. Some countries, however, <u>censor</u> everyone on what they can say anywhere, anytime. This type of <u>censorship</u> is used to control people and prevent them from complaining about the government.

centralized—*adj.* focused in one person or area. In social studies, the word is usually used to talk about power and governments. A <u>centralized</u> government gives a lot of power to one person or group of people—like a king or a single ruling party. A <u>decentralized</u> government spreads that power out to a lot of people or groups of people.

checks and balances—*n.* when talking about the U.S. government, it is the system of government branches that each limit one another's power. So the president can do some things, but Congress has a say in what he does. Same with Congress—it can do some things, but the president also has a say. The judiciary branch—the courts—have a say in everything, too, and Congress and the president have a say in who gets to be a judge.

civic—*adj.* relating to your city or town. This word is sometimes used when discussing your role as a citizen. People often say "It's your <u>civic</u> duty to vote." That just means that as a member of a community, you should take part in what is going on there.

civil disobedience—*n.* a kind of protest where you refuse to obey civil laws because you don't believe in them. <u>Civil disobedience</u> is almost always nonviolent. Martin Luther King organized sit-ins to protest "whites-only" restaurants. Black people would simply sit at a table and not leave until the cops came and took them away.

coerce—*v.* to force someone to do something by threatening them. I was <u>coerced</u> into babysitting for my sister last weekend—my dad said if I didn't, I wouldn't get the new PlayStation—ever! You may have heard of the <u>Coercive Acts</u> that England forced on the American colonies (called the Intolerable Acts by the colonists) after the Boston Tea Party.

colonize—*v.* to establish a culture in a foreign land by putting some citizens there. It often results in those citizens taking over that foreign land. Not a very nice thing to do, but it has been a common practice for many countries, including the United States.

commerce—*n.* the act of buying and selling things. When you go to Wal-Mart and buy a notebook, you are engaging in <u>commerce</u>, and so is Wal-Mart.

commodity—*n.* something that is bought or sold. Like a notebook or a car or a ton of grain. They are all <u>commodities</u>.

communism—*n.* a system where the people own the factories, farms, and other property. At least that is the <u>communist</u> ideal. In most <u>communist</u> countries so far—like Cuba and the old Soviet Union—the government "owns" the property and most of the people have little say in how everything is run.

compensation—*n.* the amount paid for goods (stuff) or services (labor). When you get paid for doing something, you are getting <u>compensation</u>. When you pay for something, you are giving <u>compensation</u>.

compromise—*n.* a settlement where each side gives up something. So if you want to watch TV after dinner but your dad wants you to wash the dishes, a <u>compromise</u> would be watching TV, and then washing the dishes afterward.

confederation—*n.* a group of people, states, or countries who join together to do something. The Confederacy in the Civil War was a <u>confederation</u> of slave-owning states in the South.

confiscate—*v.* to take away. Once my parents <u>confiscated</u> my PlayStation for one month because I got three straight Cs in English class. I suppose they had a point.

conscription—*n.* the policy of forcing citizens to fight in wars. It's also called the draft. At different points in history, America has <u>conscripted</u> people into the armed forces, usually when there was a war on. At other times, the armed forces have been made up of volunteers.

consent—*n.* permission. In social studies, it is often used to describe elected officials serving at the "<u>consent</u> of the governed." That means we put them into office by voting for them, and we can get rid of them if we want.

consequences—*n.* the results of something that happened. As a parent or teacher must have told you at some point in your life, there are <u>consequences</u> for your actions. In social studies, the word is usually used when talking about something bad that happened, like Japan bombing Pearl Harbor (<u>consequence</u>: the U.S. joined the war) or the Watergate scandal (<u>consequence</u>: Nixon resigned). But <u>consequences</u> can also stem from positive events.

constitution—*n.* the laws that govern a group of people, usually a country or a state. The U.S. <u>Constitution</u> has in it the basic

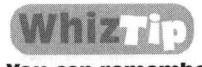

Whiz Fact

Commerce **is so important to our economy, our government has a whole section devoted to it: the Department of Commerce. Visit their website at** *www.doc.gov.*

Whiz Tip

You can remember that compromise **means an agreement because** compromise **contains the word "promise."**

Whiz Fact

Abe Lincoln **signed the act that introduced military** conscription **in 1863.**

laws that we follow in this country.

controversy—*n.* a situation where two sides have opposing views, and people have a hard time figuring out who is right. There was a huge <u>controversy</u> at my school last year when my friend Ralph refused to wear the new uniform—and his parents agreed with him! The principal called an assembly, Ralph's parents were in and out of school almost every day, Ralph was suspended, and it was in the newspaper!

covenant—*n.* a binding agreement; a compact. It's basically promising something, cross-your-heart, hope to die, stick a needle in your eye. A serious promise.

currency—*n.* a country's money. Our <u>currency</u> is dollars, the British use pounds, and the Japanese use yen.

democracy—*n.* a government where the people hold the power. We have a representative <u>democracy</u>, which means we elect representatives to do what we, the people, want them to do.

deprive—*v.* to take away. In social studies, the word is often used to talk about people being <u>deprived</u> of their rights. That means they don't have any rights to do what they want to do. When my friend Ralph's parents were against the dress code, they said Ralph was being <u>deprived</u> of his rights to dress how he wants.

despotism—*n.* rule by a despot, someone who has absolute power and can do whatever he wants. Hitler was a <u>despot</u> in Germany. Saddam Hussein is a <u>despot</u> in Iraq. There are still lots of <u>despots</u> around the world.

deter—*v.* to prevent; to stop. I try to <u>deter</u> my little sister from playing her Britney Spears CD over and over and over and . . .

diplomat—*n.* a person who represents her country while living in another country. Most countries have <u>diplomats</u> in other countries, so if something happens, say, in Mexico, the United States' <u>diplomat</u> in Mexico can make sure the United States' interests are kept in mind.

discriminate—*v.* to treat someone badly for unfair reasons. Black people have been <u>discriminated</u> against a lot in our country. Even my favorite sport, baseball, <u>discriminated</u> against black people until 1947, when Jackie Robinson became the first black man in the Major Leagues. And racial <u>discrimination</u> still exists—there may be tons of black players, but there are hardly any black managers.

dissent—*n.* disagreement. In America, you have the right to register your <u>dissent</u>, no matter what you think. It's called freedom of speech. My friend Ralph's parents had every right to register their <u>dissent</u> with the school's dress code. They lost—Ralph had to wear the uniform like the rest of us, but they still had the right to disagree.

WhizFact

The Mayflower Compact was a covenant signed by the 41 male passengers on the Mayflower, saying they would stick together.

WhizTip

To remember despotism, think of the word "despicable."

Related Word

diplomatic—adj. good at dealing with people and their problems.

DOUBLE MEANING

discriminate—v. to tell one thing from another. Example: I can't discriminate between these two cheeses: Which one is Swiss?

Social Studies

DOUBLE MEANING
diversity—n.
the variety of plants
and animals in an
ecosystem (science).

diversity—*n.* variety. In social studies, the word is usually used to talk about the <u>diversity</u> of opinions (lots of different opinions) and the <u>diversity</u> of cultures (lots of different cultures) that make up America. Some call our <u>diversity</u> a melting pot, some call it a quilt—the point is, we have a very <u>diverse</u> society.

doctrine—*n.* a set of beliefs that defines a group. The word is most often used to talk about a country's or church's <u>doctrine</u>—its set of written rules. I saw the pope on TV the other day and he was talking about Christian <u>doctrine</u> of "love thy neighbor as thyself."

Antonym

foreign—adj.
having to do
with other
countries or lands.

domestic—*adj.* having to do with home. In social studies, you may hear the phrase "<u>domestic</u> affairs"—that means things the country is dealing with at home, on its own.

dominate—*v.* to take precedence; to be most important. Combining the definition above with this one, you may have heard of "domestic affairs <u>dominating</u> Congress" or something along those lines. That means issues close to home are taking up most of the time and effort in Congress. Different issues tend to <u>dominate</u> in our culture, depending on all sorts of things: war and peace, the economy, the rights of people being respected or abused. All of these issues have <u>dominated</u> at one time or another.

due process—*n.* the established way our court system works. The phrase "You have a right to <u>due process</u>" is a big one for this country. It means no matter who you are, you get treated the same—and fairly—in our court system.

DOUBLE MEANING
economy—n. the
careful, thrifty use
of something. "She
skates with econo-
my of movement"
means she doesn't
waste any motion.

economy—*n.* the combination of goods, services, and people and how they all work together to survive. We have a <u>market economy</u>, which means the laws of supply and demand determine who makes and gets what. The other kind of <u>economy</u> is a <u>command economy</u>, in which a government determines (commands) who makes and gets what. China has a <u>command economy</u>.

eligible—*adj.* qualified; available. An <u>eligible voter</u> is someone who is qualified to vote—this person is a citizen, has registered, is old enough, etc. An <u>eligible bachelor</u> is someone who is not married or dating anyone and would make somebody a good husband. I am an <u>eligible</u> bachelor.

eloquent—*adj.* good at public speaking. If you are a politician, it helps to be <u>eloquent</u>, since you have to make so many speeches all the time. John F. Kennedy was an <u>eloquent</u> speaker, so were Ronald Reagan and Bill Clinton. But I think the most <u>eloquent</u> speaker I know is the Rock on *WWF Smackdown*. That guy can really hold an audience!

emancipation—*n.* the act of gaining freedom. Our <u>emancipation</u> from England and the <u>emancipation</u> of slaves in our country are two pivotal moments in our history.

emigrate—*v.* to leave one's home country for another. This country is made up of millions of people who have <u>emigrated</u> from distant lands to find opportunity here. Orlando Hernandez is a major league pitcher who <u>emigrated</u> from Cuba.

enforce—*v.* to make sure something takes place. Most often used in the phrase "<u>enforce</u> our laws" and "<u>enforce</u> our borders." It just means if we say we are going to do something, we will do it. My parents <u>enforce</u> their home rules by grounding me and taking away things when I break the rules.

entrepreneur—*n.* someone who takes business risks in a capitalist economy. It can be someone who bets that if she is right about a business venture, she will get rich. <u>Entrepreneurs</u> start most of the new companies in our country every year, betting the business will succeed. Steve Jobs was an <u>entrepreneur</u> when he started Apple Computer in his garage in the 1970s. Martha Stewart took an ability to make pretty doilies and turned it into a multi-million dollar empire!

epigram—*n.* a short, witty poem or saying. Ben Franklin had a bunch of them—his most famous <u>epigram</u> is probably "A penny saved is a penny earned." My dad loves that one.

expansion—*n.* growth. As in <u>territorial expansion</u>, it means a city or country keeps annexing the land that is next to it, and then the land next to that. The U.S. <u>expanded</u> from 13 states on the East Coast all the way west to California, and then picked up Alaska and Hawaii, too. Now that's what I call <u>expansion</u>.

expedition—*n.* an adventurous trip. To expand as fast as it did, the U.S. needed a lot of people to go out on <u>expeditions</u> into uncharted territory.

fascism—*n.* a government with a ruthless dictator, centralized control, and nationalist tendencies. Hitler was a <u>fascist</u>. So was Mussolini. The Allied Powers fought <u>fascism</u> in World War II and won. It's all my great-grandfather talks about!

federalism—*n.* a government with separate states that are united under one larger government. The United States (get it—*united* states) is a <u>federalist</u> system. Alexander Hamilton was a big early advocate of <u>federalism</u>.

feminism—*n.* a movement committed to getting women the same rights and opportunities as men. Women make less money than men for the same work, and our society treats them differently in many ways. <u>Feminists</u> are out to change that so everyone is equal.

forfeit—*v.* to give up; to hand over. When one commits a crime and goes to jail, he <u>forfeits</u> a lot of his rights as a citizen, like the freedom to walk around and go wherever he wants. If your baseball team doesn't show up for a game, it <u>forfeits</u> the game, and

The U.S. is called "the land of the free," so emancipation (freedom) is probably our most important ideal. That means you are lucky—but it also means lots of test questions on the subject.

Write an epigram about learning vocabulary words:

_____
_____
_____
_____

Exploration is an important subject in social studies, so whenever the teacher starts talking about expeditions, start taking notes.

WhizFact

Gloria Steinem and Betty Friedan are famous modern feminists. Elizabeth Cady Stanton is a famous suffragette—a woman who fought for women's right to vote in the early 20th century (see definition for suffrage).

loses automatically. That happened to my team when our bus broke down.

free enterprise—*n.* the economic system in which businesses can try to make a profit without the government getting in their way with lots of regulations. The United States has a <u>free enterprise</u> system.

frontier—*n.* an area of land where people don't live yet; the great unknown. The United States was once just a few states on the East Coast with a great <u>frontier</u> to its west that still "belonged" to the Native Americans. If you're a *Star Trek* fan, you've heard William Shatner say these words a million times: "Space—the final <u>frontier</u> . . . . These are the voyages of the Starship Enterprise. Its five-year mission: to explore strange new worlds, to seek out new life and new civilizations, to boldly go where no man has gone before." That's exactly how the pioneers felt when they packed up their covered wagons and headed out West.

fundamental—*adj.* basic. In this country we have certain <u>fundamental</u> rights—the rights to life, liberty, and the pursuit of happiness. Maybe you've heard of these somewhere?

futile—*adj.* useless. Lots of times people will tell you not to try, that trying is <u>futile</u>. Until the Rangers got Alex Rodriguez, I thought the team's attempts to get to the World Series were <u>futile</u>. Now, I don't think that way.

grievances—*n.* complaints. The colonists had a list of <u>grievances</u> against mother England, the biggest of which was they were getting taxed a lot. I have a list of <u>grievances</u> I gave to my mother last week, the biggest of which was my allowance needs to be higher. The colonists rebelled. I hope my mom gets the hint!

hardship—*n.* a bad thing; an obstacle. The first English colonists endured lots of <u>hardships</u>, like starving, having no shelter, and dying of diseases.

hazardous—*adj.* dangerous. You've probably seen this word in ads for cigarettes: "CAUTION: Cigarette smoking may be <u>hazardous</u> to your health." Being an early colonist was also definitely <u>hazardous</u> to one's health (see the definition for <u>hardship</u> for more on this).

humanitarian—*adj.* helpful to humans. You've probably heard of the U.S. sending <u>humanitarian</u> aid to countries that need help. That basically means we send food and medicine. A couple years ago my school had a can and clothes drive and sent <u>humanitarian</u> aid to hurricane victims in Florida.

immigration—*n.* the act of coming from a foreign country to live in a new country. America has grown in population over the years mainly due to <u>immigration</u>. The country practically begged people to <u>immigrate</u> here so it could push west over the frontier

List three things you once thought were futile:

1. _____
2. _____
3. _____

Write down a hardship you have gone through:

_____
_____
_____

**DOUBLE MEANING
humanitarian—n.** someone who is known for his work helping mankind. Jonas Salk was a great humanitarian—he discovered the vaccine for polio.

and fill up all of its land with new citizens.

impartial—*adj.* fair. Judges and juries are supposed to be impartial. That means they just go by the facts. Like Judge Judy on TV—she is an impartial judge who listens to all the facts, then she reams the person who is guilty.

impeachment—*n.* charging an elected official with doing something wrong. President Clinton was impeached a few years ago. It was only the second time in the history of the country a president was impeached. Clinton's impeachment hearings dominated the news for weeks.

imperialism—*n.* rule by an empire. A few hundred years ago, imperialism was the way to go. There was the Roman Empire, the Spanish Empire, the German Empire. These imperial governments would go out and conquer a bunch of countries so they could expand their empires. Of course America was part of the British Empire—imperial Britain—at one point.

impose—*v.* to force. My Spanish teacher imposed a "no English" rule last week in class, so no one could speak English in her class the whole week! If you did, you had to put your head on your desk for five minutes. It was really funny watching everyone mess up and put their heads on their desk.

inalienable—*adj.* unable to be taken away; unable to be separated from. Most often linked to Americans' inalienable rights of life, liberty, and the pursuit of happiness. One way to remember this word is to think about the word "alien." Space aliens are beings from other planets. So something that is INalienable is something that is NOT something from another planet.

inaugurate—*v.* to have a ceremony where a politician gets installed in office. George W. Bush was inaugurated in 2001 after a bitter election battle against Al Gore.

indigenous—*adj.* native. The people who are originally from a country are called the country's indigenous people. Native Americans are indigenous to North America—everyone else who lives in this country came here from somewhere else or is descended from someone who did.

inevitable—*adj.* going to happen; unavoidable. It is inevitable that you are going to have to take tests, so you might as well just get used to them. When something is unavoidable, my grandfather always says, "It's as inevitable as death and taxes." I have my own expression, "It's as inevitable as death, taxes, and the TAAS."

influence—*n.* the power to change something. The United States has incredible influence around the world. In 1936, a man named Dale Carnegie wrote a book called *How to Win Friends and Influence People*, and it became one of the best-selling books of all time because, well, that's what everyone wants, right?

inhabitants—*n.* people who live somewhere. You are an inhab-

Whiz Quiz

Who was the first president to be impeached? Hint: it wasn't Bill Clinton.

DOUBLE MEANING
impose—v. to butt in. You may have heard people say "I don't mean to impose, but . . ." and then they go ahead and impose.

itant of Texas. Prince Charles is an <u>inhabitant</u> of England.

innovation—*n.* a brand new way of doing something or a new device that is better than how it used to be. The electric guitar was an <u>innovation</u> that allowed bands to play louder. Before the electric guitar, the only way to play loud was on an acoustic guitar aimed at a microphone.

instability—*n.* the state of being unsteady and insecure. When things are up in the air, when they can go one way or the other—that is <u>instability</u>. For example, there is <u>instability</u> on a baseball team when the players don't like the manager, and the manager doesn't like the players. Who is right—the players who say the manager is stupid or the manager who says the players are terrible? Who do you side with? All these questions lead to <u>instability</u>. It's the same with a country when there is <u>instability</u>. Usually, there is <u>instability</u> when there is a change in leaders. Maybe the army liked the old leader better, so they won't listen to the new leader. That leads to <u>instability</u>.

institution—*n.* a really well- known or well- established organization or person. There are real <u>institutions</u> like colleges (<u>institutions</u> for higher learning) and hospitals (health <u>institutions</u>). There are also people who are known as <u>institutions</u>—like Bill Cosby is a comedy <u>institution</u>, and Michael Jordan is a basketball <u>institution</u>. They are just SO IMPORTANT to their fields, they are <u>institutions</u>.

insurgent—*n.* a person who revolts against authority. When you watch newscasters, you may hear them talk about "rebel <u>insurgents</u>" in other countries, and then show some guys with machine guns running around in the woods fighting against government forces.

insurrection—*n.* revolt against the people in charge. The word is used in the Declaration of Independence to describe the king of England's treatment of the colonies: "He has excited domestic <u>insurrections</u> amongst us." That means the colonists thought the king was turning them against each other.

integration—*n.* the creation of one group by combining different groups; having people of all different races living together instead of apart. Our country was segregated—white people and black people were separated from each other until the 1950s and 1960s, when segregation was made illegal. Now we are an <u>integrated</u> society—people of all races are allowed to live side by side.

integrity—*n.* honesty; trustworthiness. People who do what they say they are going to do have <u>integrity</u>. People who lie do not have <u>integrity</u>. I think Justin Timberlake has <u>integrity</u> for staying with 'N Sync, even though he could go solo and make millions.

interdependent—*adj.* depending on each other. Countries are getting more and more <u>interdependent</u>. Lots of countries rely on us for corn; we rely on lots of countries for oil; and everyone relies on France for French fries.

intervene—*v.* to butt in. I had to <u>intervene</u> on the playground last week when my friend Ralph and that jerk Frankie got into a fight. I was able to keep them apart until the teacher came.

intolerant—*adj.* unable to accept views one doesn't agree with. There are lots of <u>intolerant</u> people in the world—people who don't like other people just because they are different. Don't be <u>intolerant</u>. It will just make you mean.

invasion—*n.* the attack on another country and the taking over of their land. The D-Day <u>invasion</u> of Normandy in World War II in 1944 is the largest, and one of the most famous, <u>invasions</u> ever. The Allied forces caught the Germans by surprise and ended up driving them out of France.

isolate—*v.* to separate from everything else. When I was in kindergarten, I was a big spaz. Sometimes I got so hyper my teacher had to <u>isolate</u> me at nap time—she put up big dividers so I couldn't see the rest of the kids and they couldn't see me.

jeopardy—*n.* peril; danger. Think of the game show *Jeopardy*. If you go on that show, you are in <u>jeopardy</u> of looking really stupid if you can't answer any questions.

judicious—*adj.* showing good judgment. When I am pitching a baseball game, I have to be <u>judicious</u> in how hard I throw the ball. If I throw it way too hard, I can't last very long because my arm gets tired.

jurisdiction—*n.* an area of authority. The word <u>jurisdiction</u> is often used to talk about the courts having <u>jurisdiction</u> over a case. That means the case happened in a court's physical area. So if someone robbed someone in Oliveras County, the case would be tried in the <u>jurisdiction</u> of Oliveras County.

lame duck—*n.* a politician who has some time left in her term, but her replacement has already been elected. So she is still doing her job, but she has already been voted out. That means she has no power, and she's basically just keeping the seat warm for her successor.

legislation—*n.* proposed laws. In the U.S. government, Congress writes and votes on <u>legislation</u>.

limit—*n.* the end; the most; the end of the line. My <u>limit</u> on chicken wings is 28. I have never eaten more than 28, although I have tried many times.

loyalist—*n.* someone who is loyal to a leader or government. British <u>loyalists</u> who lived in the American colonies were against the colonies breaking from mother England.

WhizTip

Think of the word "depend" to remember interdependent.

WhizTip

To remember jurisdiction, think of the word "jury." A case's jurisdiction is wherever a jury would be seated to try the case.

WhizQuiz

Go to *www.house.gov* and find a piece of legislation Congress is working on now.

mandate—*n.* the right to do something. In elections, when voters pick someone overwhelmingly, that politician has a mandate. That means the voters have told him—with their votes—that he can do what he wants because they agree with his plan. When a politician wins in a landslide (see the Related Word) he has a mandate from the voters. When there is a close election (like when George W. Bush barely beat Al Gore in 2000), there is not a mandate because lots of people voted for the guy who lost.

manifest destiny—*n.* a policy of imperialist expansion that says a country can take over another country because God says so. Imperialist countries like England took over other countries using this concept of manifest destiny. The United States took over lots of its western lands by using this concept of manifest destiny. Manifest destiny is bad. It's basically just an excuse to take over a country.

mercenary—*n.* a professional soldier. Mercenaries fight for whomever pays them to fight. There's even a magazine for mercenaries called *Soldier of Fortune*. Get it? They *soldier* so they can make a *fortune*.

microcosm—*n.* a detail of something bigger; a miniature version of something big. New York City is often called a microcosm of the world because there are immigrants from just about every country living there, speaking just about every language known to man.

migration—*n.* the movement from one place to another. In the past 20 years, there has been a migration of people in this country from cold places like New York to warm places like Texas.

militant—*adj.* combative; warring. Some countries have militant histories, ours included.

moderate—*adj.* not extreme. Moderate temperatures are not too hot and not too cold. Moderate politicians are not too liberal and not too conservative.

modify—*v.* to change; to alter. The U.S. Constitution is modified by adding on amendments.

motivation—*n.* the reason you do something. My motivation for writing all these definitions and exercises is to help you do better on your tests.

municipal—*adj.* related to a city or a town. You probably have heard of a municipal government and a municipal school system and municipal courts. That just means those things are located in a city—whatever city that may be.

mutual—*adj.* sharing something in common. When something is done for the mutual benefit of all, that means everyone benefits. When Justin Timberlake and Britney Spears are seen in public together, they mutually benefit. All of her fans start to like him, and all of his fans start to like her.

nationalism—*n.* loyalty to one's country. <u>Nationalism</u> is a good thing when it means you really like your country and are proud of it. <u>Nationalism</u> is a bad thing when it means you really like your country but hate all the other countries. Most often these days, when you hear about <u>nationalism</u>, it's when one country is beating up on another one out of a feeling of <u>nationalism</u>.

naturalization—*n.* the granting of citizenship to someone. The word is most often used when discussing the INS—the Immigration and <u>Naturalization</u> Service. That is the agency that helps people immigrate to this country and become citizens. A <u>naturalized</u> citizen is someone who immigrated here and became a citizen later.

negotiate—*v.* to discuss something with the goal of reaching an agreement. Throughout history there have basically been two ways to solve disagreements—to fight or to <u>negotiate</u>. <u>Negotiating</u> is better, because nobody gets hurt.

nemesis—*n.* sworn enemy. The Joker is Batman's <u>nemesis</u>. Lex Luthor is Superman's <u>nemesis</u>. Christina Aguilera is Britney Spears' <u>nemesis</u>. The Soviet Union used to be the United States' <u>nemesis</u>.

neutral—*adj.* not taking sides. Lots of times, when two countries go to war, other countries remain <u>neutral</u>. That means they aren't taking sides in the war—they are staying out of it. The United States was <u>neutral</u> in World War II until Japan bombed Pearl Harbor.

nullify—*v.* to void; to take something back. Sometimes, after an agreement has been negotiated, something happens and the agreement gets <u>nullified</u>. That means all the negotiating was wasted, because the agreement that was reached doesn't count. It happens all the time in baseball when a team is trying to make a trade, but the trade gets <u>nullified</u> when one of the players doesn't pass his physical.

obligation—*n.* a promise to do something; a sense of duty. I feel it is my <u>obligation</u> to help you improve your vocabulary. I promised you in the introduction to this book that I would, so I am!

obstacle—*n.* something that gets in the way. You have probably been in a race through an <u>obstacle</u> course at some point. My main <u>obstacle</u> at school is I have a hard time paying attention, but I'm working on it.

opportunity—*n.* chance. The United States has been called "the land of <u>opportunity</u>." And my dad is always saying "When <u>opportunity</u> knocks—open the door!" He loves that one.

opposition—*n.* someone who is against someone else. It looks like the Texas Rangers' main <u>opposition</u> this year as they try to get to the World Series is going to be the New York Yankees.

oppress—*v.* to keep somebody down. This country has a histo-

WhizFact

The scientist Albert Einstein once said "Nationalism is an infantile sickness. It is the measles of the human race."

WhizFact

Millions of immigrants were naturalized at Ellis Island in New York Harbor in the early 1900s.

WhizQuiz

Name your nemesis!

Synonym

impartial—adj. fair. (See the definition in social studies.)

WhizQuiz

Name your favorite team's main opposition:

ry of <u>oppressing</u> black people and women. Luckily, that <u>oppression</u> isn't nearly as bad now as it used to be.

orator—*n.* someone who gives speeches. It is important for a politician to be a good <u>orator</u>, because he has to give speeches that convince people to vote for him. President Bush is NOT a good <u>orator</u>—he can barely string together two sentences.

partisan—*n.* a supporter of a political party; a supporter of a cause. You have probably heard of "<u>partisan</u> politics" in Washington, DC. That means our two major political parties—the Democrats and Republicans—are more interested in getting their way then getting something done. Being a <u>partisan</u>—a supporter of their party—is more important than doing what they were elected to do. That's kind of bad.

perpetrator—*n.* someone who is guilty of something. More specifically, a perpetrator is usually someone who commits—<u>perpetrates</u>—a crime. In cop-speak, <u>perpetrators</u> of crimes are called "perps." Just watch an episode of any police drama on TV—the cops say "perp" every other sentence.

persecute—*v.* to oppress. The Nazis <u>persecuted</u> Jews in World War II. The Romans <u>persecuted</u> Christians for hundreds of years. European colonists <u>persecuted</u> Native Americans for hundreds of years. Unfortunately, the history of mankind is filled with <u>persecution</u>.

petition—*n.* a formal request to a government or another authority. You have probably signed a <u>petition</u> at some point in your life. Last year I signed a <u>petition</u> to end the dress code at my school, but it didn't work—we still have a dress code!

pivotal—*adj.* the most important. The <u>pivotal</u> moment of my last baseball game was when the other team had the bases loaded and I struck out their best hitter. That's what I call <u>pivotal</u>.

posterity—*n.* future generations. Sometimes presidents do things for <u>posterity</u>, which means they do things so they will be remembered as a good president by future generations. President Clinton made a bunch of national forests untouchable by loggers so he would be remembered by <u>posterity</u> as a president who helped the environment.

pragmatist—*n.* someone who is practical. A <u>pragmatist</u> tends to support things he thinks can actually be done. For example, a <u>pragmatist</u> would be satisfied if a last-place team just improved a little, and maybe the next year made it to the middle of the pack. He wouldn't expect the team to go from last place to first place in one year, because that wouldn't be practical.

preservation—*n.* protection from destruction. This word is used most often when people are talking about <u>preserving</u> old buildings in their town (historic <u>preservation</u>), and when people are talking about preserving the environment (environmental <u>preservation</u>).

primary source—*n.* a first-hand record of an event. I was doing a report on how the pitcher Nolan Ryan got so good. Some of my primary sources were two letters that he wrote to his dad and tapes of three games he pitched way back in the 1970s.

principles—*n.* ideals; beliefs. A person who has principles is a person who does what he thinks is right, no matter what the consequences. Martin Luther King, Jr. had principles. So did Che Guevara.

productive—*adj.* able to produce a lot of stuff. A productive writer writes a lot of books and articles. A productive farmer harvests a lot of crops. A productive hitter hits a lot of extra-base hits and gets a lot of RBIs.

profit—*n.* in business, the money left over after you subtract the costs of making something that you sell. If it costs a company $20 to make a CD player and they sell it for $50, their profit is $30.

prohibit—*v.* to not allow; to forbid. Laws are basically created to prohibit bad behavior like drunk driving and stealing.

prosecute—*v.* to bring a legal case against someone. Famous people are always getting prosecuted for breaking the law. Puff Daddy got prosecuted for carrying an illegal weapon and bribing people. Jennifer Lopez was with him when he got arrested, but she didn't get prosecuted. I wonder why?

prosperity—*n.* success and riches. America is known for being a land of prosperity—there are a lot of people in this country who are rich and middle class. Many countries have no prosperity at all—everyone is poor.

provisional—*adj.* temporary. Lots of times you will hear about provisional governments. That means the government is only in place for a short time until a permanent government is installed.

provoke—*v.* to anger; to egg on. Many animals are quite peaceful until they are provoked. Most bears won't even pay you any attention, but if you provoke them by poking them with a stick or shooting at them, you are in big trouble.

public domain—*n.* land that's owned by the state or government instead of by a person. Theoretically, that means all taxpayers "own" and can use the land. In the West, a lot of livestock graze on land that's public domain.

purchasing power—*n.* the ability of people to buy things. The one main thing that affects a person's purchasing power is how much money he makes.

qualifications—*n.* skills. A person needs only two qualifications to be president of the United States—to be born in the United States and to be over 35 years old. That's it.

radical—*n.* someone who works for political or social revolution. Our country has a complicated relationship with radicals.

Whiz Fact

Shakespeare was a very productive writer, writing around 40 plays and hundreds of poems in his lifetime.

Related Word

profitable—adj. able to make a profit.

Related Word

prosperous—adj. rich.

DOUBLE MEANING

public domain—n. books, articles, and products that aren't protected by a copyright. (Note: This book is NOT public domain!)

Social Studies

WhizFact

Famous radicals include crazy writer Abbie Hoffman, presidential assassin Lee Harvey Oswald, and President Thomas Jefferson, who was a big fan of revolutions.

DOUBLE MEANING

ration—n. quantities of food.

When we were colonies breaking from England, we were the radicals, breaking the law. Now, as the most powerful nation in the world, we generally look down on radicals. And as a country based on the rule of law, revolution is not really our cup of tea. Just look at the famous radicals our country has had to see how complicated our relationship with them is.

ratify—v. to pass. After a law is written, it has to be ratified by both houses of Congress—the House of Representatives and the Senate, before it is signed (or vetoed) by the president.

ration—v. to give out in restricted amounts, usually during wartime, to conserve resources. Food and fuel are often rationed during wartime so more resources can be devoted to fighting the battles.

rebellion—n. a revolt against authority. Have you noticed how many words there are in this section that basically mean "revolt" and "rebel"? It is an important subject when it comes to the history of our country. Not only was rebellion how the United States broke from England, rebels have qualities that we as Americans value—rebels do what they think is right, no matter what anyone thinks.

Reconstruction—n. the period after the Civil War when the South was controlled by the federal government, before those states were readmitted to the Union (1865-1877).

recruit—v. to get someone to join something. The most obvious place you'll see this word is when people are talking about recruiting soldiers to join the armed forces. But people are also recruited to join the soccer team, the PTA, and to attend a particular college.

reform—v. to change for the better. One of the great things about our government is that if a law—or the government—doesn't work, we can reform it by voting for representatives who want to change things, too.

regional—adj. area-specific. My baseball team plays in a regional tournament every year. That's the big tournament where all the teams from the region of southwest Texas play. The games are called the regionals.

Related Word

regulation—n. a rule restricting behavior or actions.

regulate—v. to limit. The government regulates all kinds of things. The most important may be the toxic emissions from cars and power plants. The government regulates those emissions by setting limits the companies must not exceed. If the company doesn't follow those regulations, the company gets fined.

relative—adj. in comparison. For example, relative to Shaquille O'Neal, I am a tiny bug. But relative to a tiny bug, I am a huge skyscraper. Get it?

repeal—v. to take back; to rescind. Sometimes a law is repealed because is was really a bad, bad idea. One of the reasons the colonies broke from England was that England wouldn't <u>repeal</u> tax laws that were really hard on the colonies.

representation—*n.* the act of representing something or someone. In the phrase "taxation without <u>representation</u>," it means not having <u>representatives</u> in the government looking out for your interests. The main reason the colonies broke with England was that they were being taxed, but had no say at all in how much they were taxed and why.

republic—*n.* a government where the people elect representatives to do their bidding. The United States is a <u>republic</u>. Texas used to be its own <u>republic</u> before it became part of the United States.

resolute—*adj.* firm; unwavering. I am <u>resolute</u> in my view that the Texas Rangers are the best team in baseball, no matter what their actual record is.

responsibilities—*n.* duties; things you have to do. As citizens of the United States, we have a ton of rights, but we also have a ton of <u>responsibilities</u>. Those include being tolerant of one another; helping those less fortunate than ourselves; obeying the laws meant to protect everyone equally; and driving on the right side of the road, not the left.

restrain—*v.* to hold back. For example, I had to <u>restrain</u> my sister when my friend Ralph called her the Texas Twit. She was going to rock his world! In American history, the New England <u>Restraining</u> Act was enacted by King Charles II in 1775. It <u>restrained</u> a handful of colonies from trading with anyone, and it made those colonies mad.

retaliation—*n.* the act of striking back after you get attacked. It is not good to start a fight, but sometimes <u>retaliation</u> is necessary (see what my sister did in the definition above). Lincoln issued the Order of <u>Retaliation</u> in 1863 saying that if the South violated the rules of war by killing or enslaving captured Union soldiers, the Union would <u>retaliate</u> by doing the same to their soldiers.

revenue—*n.* money made. Government gets its <u>revenue</u> from taxes. Companies get their <u>revenue</u> by selling things. I get my <u>revenue</u> from my allowance and mowing lawns.

secede—*v.* to break away from a unit. The South <u>seceded</u> from the United States in 1861. That's what started the Civil War, because President Lincoln would not let them do it without a fight. The South's <u>secession</u> was a pivotal moment in this country's history.

secondary source—*n.* a summary or an account of an event or person. When I wrote my report on Nolan Ryan, I used two <u>secondary sources</u>: a *Sports Illustrated* article about him and his biography on *majorleaguebaseball.com*.

segregation—*n.* the separation of people who are different.

Antonym

monarchy—**n.**
a government ruled by a king or queen.

Antonym

surrender—**v.**
to give up.

37

Social Studies

Antonym

integration—n.
the combining of
groups of people.

Blacks were <u>segregated</u> from white society for years in this country. In some churches, women and men are <u>segregated</u>, with women sitting on one side, men on the other. Boys are often <u>segregated</u> from girls in gym class. <u>Segregation</u> keeps people apart.

siege—*n*. in war, a sustained attack. In World War I, troops were under a continuous state of <u>siege</u>. The fighting never stopped as the soldiers on both sides dug trenches and refused to give an inch.

significant—*adj*. important, but a little less important than "pivotal." The Civil War was a pivotal moment in our history. The War with Iraq was a <u>significant</u> moment. Important, but not as much. Looked at another way, signing Alex Rodriguez was a pivotal moment in Texas Rangers baseball history. Signing John Wetteland, a pretty good pitcher, was only <u>significant</u>.

sovereign—*n*. a king or queen. We don't have any sovereigns in our country. England still has its <u>sovereigns</u>, but they don't have any power anymore. They are just symbols of England's past.

stereotype—*n*. a judgment based on oversimple assumptions. You are using a <u>stereotype</u> when you think a person or group of people are a certain way for no real reason. For example, Italian Americans are often <u>stereotyped</u> as being in the Mafia. Blonde women are often <u>stereotyped</u> as being ditzy. Obviously, a <u>stereotype</u> has nothing to do with an individual person. It's just a lazy way to form opinions of people.

WhizTip

To remember
subversive means
"undermining"
remember sub
means "under."

subversive—*adj*. undermining. As part of preparing for a war against France, Thomas Jefferson signed the Alien and Sedition Acts, which outlawed <u>subversive</u> behavior, like criticizing the government. Now we can criticize the government as much as we want.

succession—*n*. the process of following in order. There is a <u>succession</u> of kings and queens in the history of most European nations. Sometimes the <u>succession</u> went smoothly. Sometimes, it was bloody.

WhizTip

To remember
suffrage,
remember
people "suffer"
when they don't
have the right
to vote.

suffrage—*n*. the right to vote. Women gained <u>suffrage</u> in this country in 1920. Eighteen-year-olds gained <u>suffrage</u> after the Vietnam War when they argued that if they could go to war, why couldn't they vote?

sympathizers—*n*. people who agree with something and want to help; people who are <u>sympathetic</u> to a person or a cause. Usually in American history, the word is used in the term "communist <u>sympathizers</u>," which means people who agreed with the communists and helped them out in the early 20th century.

tariffs—*n*. taxes on imports and exports. High <u>tariffs</u> on the colonies' imports and exports made colonists' mad at England. You know what happened next.

temperance—*n.* the act of not drinking alcohol. There was a <u>temperance</u> movement in the United States in the early 20th century that made drinking alcohol illegal. That was when gangsters like Al Capone made millions selling illegal booze.

transcend—*v.* to surpass; to overcome. Sometimes you have to <u>transcend</u> your limitations to reach your goals. If your vocabulary is a limitation for you, this book should help you <u>transcend</u> that obstacle.

Treasury—*n.* the part of the government in charge of the money supply. Our <u>Treasury Department</u> makes sure there is enough, but not too much, money floating around to keep the economy moving.

truce—*n.* a stop in the fighting. Sometimes in a war the sides just call a <u>truce</u> without anyone declaring victory. They just stop fighting because they are tired of seeing their people killed.

unanimous—*adj.* being in complete, 100 percent agreement. In a <u>unanimous</u> decision, everyone votes the same way. When we took a vote from the students at school about our dress code, the students voted <u>unanimously</u> to repeal it.

unity—*n.* the act of being together. Our country is called the United States because all of the states have a <u>unity</u> of purpose: they all want the country to succeed, and they all support its general goals and direction.

urban—*adj.* related to the city. Lots of big cities around the country have been undergoing <u>urban</u> renewal, which means they are working to improve the quality of their inner cities and downtown areas. I was in Austin last summer and it was undergoing <u>urban</u> renewal—there was a new museum being built downtown and lots of shops were opening back up.

usurp—*v.* to take over; to seize power. Many times members of Congress have tried to <u>usurp</u> the authority of the president by passing legislation that lessens the president's power. Sometimes they have prevailed, sometimes they have failed. Once I tried to <u>usurp</u> my parents and told my sister she could stay up late when they told her she had to go to sleep. I got in trouble for that one.

utopia—*n.* a perfect world. Many systems of government promise their followers a <u>utopia</u> on Earth. I think Texas is the closest anyone has come to <u>utopia</u> yet!

verdict—*n.* a decision in a court case. It is the job of a jury to reach a <u>verdict</u> in a case. When members of a jury don't reach a verdict, it's called a "hung jury."

veteran—*n.* someone who has fought in a war. We celebrate <u>Veterans</u> Day to remember the people who have fought in all of our wars. My great-grandfather is a <u>veteran</u>—he fought in World War II.

veto—*n.* rejection of a proposal. In our government, a <u>veto</u> is a

Whiz Quiz
Name a limitation you have had to transcend in your life:
_____
_____

Related Word
majority—adj. In a majority vote, more than 50 percent of the people vote one way, but not everybody.

Antonym
rural—adj. related to the countryside.

Whiz Tip
Fruitopia is a fruit drink that plays off the word utopia: Fruitopia is supposed to be the "perfect" fruit drink.

president's vote against legislation passed by Congress. Presidents often <u>veto</u> legislation they don't agree with.

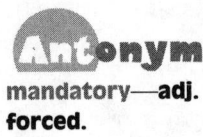

mandatory—*adj.* **forced.**

voluntary—*adj.* of one's own choice, with no outside force. Our armed forces are now <u>voluntary</u>, but in times of war, you can be forced to fight. At my school, joining band or sports is <u>voluntary</u>, but everyone must take math and science.

WhizWords

communism
democracy
despotism
fascism
federalism
imperialism
republic

Social Studies

Government

I was over at my great-grandfather's assisted living complex the other day, and he was going on and on about World War II. He's a good guy, but when you get him started on World War II, you might as well pull up a chair because you're going to be there for awhile. Anyway, he was talking about **fascists** and **communists** and all of these different kinds of governments I have only heard of in social studies class.

It made me realize that I wrongly assumed that all countries are **democracies** like ours. When my great-grandfather was growing up, Germany had a **fascist** government; Russia was part of the Soviet Union and was a **communist** country; **imperialism** was the favorite kind of government for all kinds of kings in the Middle East; and the African countries that weren't run as colonies by France and England were run by **despots.**

My great-grandfather lived in crazy times! Today, the Middle East oil countries are still pretty much all run by kings, and Africa is still full of **despots,** but lots of the rest of the countries—like Germany and Japan— have gone **democratic.**

Related Word

nationalism—n. **You really like your country, and hate all the other countries. Nazi Germany was based on intense** nationalism. **The Nazis were going to rule the whole world, and kill anyone they thought was unworthy of being a member of the Third Reich.**

IDENTIFY THE GOVERNMENT TYPE EXERCISE

Following are some countries that have gone through some big changes over the years. If you don't know what kind of government was in place on the dates I give you (and from the hints in my descriptions), do some research in the library or on the Internet to find out. You will be very surprised by what you find.

Country	Year	Government?
England	1714	King George I assumes the throne
Texas	1836	Texas is an independent republic.
United States	1897	William McKinley was elected out 25th president.
Germany	1935	Hitler rules with an iron fist.
Jordan	1953	King Hussein assumes his hereditary position.
Cambodia	1976	The totalitarian Khmer Rouge wreaked havoc.
England	1979	Margaret Thatcher was elected the first woman prime minister.

Whenever you hear about a country in the news that you don't know anything about, do some research and figure out what kind of government it has. I've been doing this for the last few months whenever I hear about a country in Africa or Asia, because I don't know very much about those two continents. It is really scary how few democracies there are out there!

WhizWords

agitator
anarchy
insurgent
insurrection
militant
radical
rebellion
subversive

Social Studies
Revolution

Related Word

utopia—n.
a perfect world.
Many rebellions
are led by agitators
who promise their
followers utopia.

Rebellion is a tricky subject. Whether a revolution is good or bad often depends on what side you are on. For example, the colonists' **rebellion** against mother England is the only reason the United States of America even exists. And our democracy was a big experiment at the time. The fact that it worked basically opened the door for democracies everywhere. So there—a "good" **insurrection**.

But if you watch the news every day, you see **revolutions** all over the place, and they are not pretty, and the result of the **rebellion** is not always good.

THE HISTORY OF REBELLION EXERCISE

From our history and the continuing events in many countries, you can see why words about rebellion and revolution are so important to know. To get a better handle on the vocabulary often used to describe revolution and revolutionaries, I want you to write one short essay comparing and contrasting any two rebellions. For your convenience, I'll go ahead and list some of the more interesting rebellions of the past few hundred years:

1. **1776: Colonists Rebel Against England**
2. **1789: The French rebel against King Louis XVI**
3. **1917: Russians rebel against the czar**
4. **1956: Communists in Cuba revolt**

Be sure to use all of the "Revolution" words in the essay, and try to squeeze in the Related Word as well. If, when you have completed your exercise, you want to make sure you are comfortable with the words, compare two of the remaining rebellions to test yourself.

Related Word

sympathizer—n.
a person who agrees
with something
and wants to help.
A sympathizer might
participate in
subversive activities
to support a
radical cause.

WhizWords

abolitionist
bias
discriminate
emancipation
feminism
integration
intolerant
oppress
persecute
segregation
stereotype
suffrage

Social Studies

Inequality

People rebel because they feel they are being **oppressed** or **discriminated** against. **Feminists** fight for the rights of women every day because women don't have the same rights as men. **Abolitionists** fought for the freedom of slaves, who didn't have any rights at all. In fact, the history of our country is filled with situations where individuals had to overcome **bias** and **discrimination.** And our country is called the land of the free! So you can just imagine what life is like in countries where equality isn't even talked about, much less strived for.

Luckily in the United States, we have made great strides. There is pretty much universal **suffrage** now—everyone over the age of 18 can vote. Our public schools, public places, and the military are all **integrated**, too. Not long ago, white people and black people were **segregated.**

Even so, there is still a lot of **intolerance** around. Lots of the advances in equality have happened in the past 20 or 30 years, but old habits die hard. So some people still use **stereotypes** to judge those who are different than they are.

Related Word

diversity—n. variety. Diversity and integration can help people learn that stereotypes and biases are shallow and stupid.

SUFFRAGE FOR FASHION MODELS EXERCISE

The fight for equal rights is a serious business. People have given their lives so that others may have equal opportunity. However, for this exercise, let's lighten things up a little. Pretend there is only one group left in this country that is being discriminated against: skinny fashion models. Now, get a pencil and paper and write a make-believe history about how skinny fashion models go from being segregated, discriminated against, and not having the right to vote to being integrated, having equal rights, and having suffrage in the year 2050. Use as many of the words above as you can.

ESSAY:

The History of Skinny Fashion Models' Fight
For Suffrage in the 21st Century

WhizWords

ambition
carpetbagger
civic
impeachment
inaugurate
lame duck
mandate
partisan

Social Studies
Politics

The best way to build your vocabulary is to read, read, and read some more. Newspapers are a good source of reading material. You'll find new information about things you're interested in every day.

Did you pay attention to the 2000 presidential race? When it started I didn't pay too much attention. But my dad is such a big Bush fan, he made me go to some rallies, and I started to get excited. And then the election! Nobody won! It took them about a month to figure out who the next president was going to be. It was the first time I stopped thinking about baseball and started thinking about something else outside of school.

The election got me started reading the political stories in the newspaper. That's when I started to realize there was a ton of words I didn't know very well. For example—**carpetbagger.** Have you ever heard that word? And **lame duck.** I mean, what do ducks have to do with politics, especially ducks that waddle with a limp?

Apparently a lot, because **lame duck** and **carpetbagger** kept coming up over and over again, along with **impeachment, mandate,** and **partisan.** It's no wonder they are important to know for the TAAS and other tests. If you know these words, you will be a more informed citizen, and, therefore, hopefully vote for the right person more often. At least that's the idea.

READ THE POLITICS PAGE EXERCISE

Keep Word Whiz handy. Pick up the latest copy of your local newspaper. Not the free handout you get at the grocery store with all of the used cars for sale—the real thing. Start with the Sunday paper if you can—it's usually about twice as thick. Now find the stories about local and national politics and start reading. Whenever you see one of the WhizWords above, underline it. Write down the number of times each word appears.

Keep doing this for one week. That's right—read the political stories every day for one week. People may think you are crazy, but do it anyway. You can still read the sports page and the comics (my personal favorites), but read political news first. Underline, count, write the "Politics" words listed above in this chart.

	Day 1	Day 2	Day 3	Day 4	Day 5	Day 6	Day 7
ambition							
carpetbagger							
civic							
impeachment							
inaugurate							
lame duck							
mandate							
partisan							

Which word won? Which came in second? Make sure you know the Top Three like the back of your hand, and make sure you know the rest of 'em like the front of your hand.

WhizWords

boom and bust economy
capital
capitalist
capitalize
commerce
commodity
economy
entrepreneur
free enterprise
profit
purchasing power

Social Studies

Economics

Did I say this country was all about freedom and equality? Just ask Alex Rodriguez, who signed a contract with the Texas Rangers for over $250 million, what this country is all about, and he might say "Show me the money!"

I mean, I love Alex Rodriguez. He is definitely the best shortstop in the league. But $250 million? I think he gets like $50,000 for each at bat or something like that. I only get $10 a week for my allowance! Maybe Alex can spare a few hundred bucks?

No wonder tests spend so much time on **economics** and **capitalism.** As a citizen of the richest country on the planet, it is important that you know how **capitalism** works so you can carry on the tradition. Especially if you end up being Alex Rodriguez!

READ THE BUSINESS PAGE EXERCISE

This exercise is basically a repeat of the politics exercise. After you get done with your week of reading the political stories in the paper, I want you to do a week of reading the business stories in the paper. I know—and you thought it couldn't get any more boring than politics!

Here's your chart for the week:

	Day 1	Day 2	Day 3	Day 4	Day 5	Day 6	Day 7
boom and bust							
capital							
capitalist							
capitalize							
commerce							
commodity							
economy							
entrepreneur							
free enterprise							
profit							
purchasing power							

Again, know the Top Three like the back of your hand and the rest like the front of your hand.

Chapter 3

Math

angle—*n*. the figure formed when two lines meet at a point. There are three kinds of <u>angles</u>: acute (less than 90⁰), obtuse (greater than 90⁰), and right (90⁰).

acute angle   obtuse angle   right angle

angle—*n*. oh yeah, there are two more kinds of angles—complementary and supplementary. <u>Complementary angles</u> add up to 90⁰. <u>Supplementary angles</u> add up to 180⁰.

area—*n*. the amount of surface on a figure. For example, a rectangle's <u>area</u> is length x width. A triangle's <u>area</u> is 1/2 base x height. A circle's <u>area</u> is πr^2. Just remember: <u>area</u> is the amount of space inside the lines.

average—*n*. what you get when you add up a bunch of numbers and then divide by the number of numbers you added up. The <u>average</u> of the numbers 9, 13, 28, 72, 83 = (9 + 13 + 28 + 72 + 83) ÷ 5 = 205 ÷ 5 = 41. So 41 is the <u>average</u> of those five numbers.

bisect—*v*. to divide into two usually equal parts. In math, a line or a point usually <u>bisects</u> another line. It cuts that line in two. Once in science we had to dissect a frog, and I had to <u>bisect</u> its brain—I actually cut its brain in half. I almost fainted.

capacity—*n*. the amount something can hold. For example, my dad's Nissan Stanza's gas tank has a <u>capacity</u> of 12 gallons of gas.

circumference—*n*. the length of the boundary of a circle. If you took a circle and straightened out the line that surrounds it and measured it, that's the <u>circumference</u>. The formula to find a circle's <u>circumference</u> is $2\pi r$, with *r* standing for *radius*.

congruent—*adj*. having the same shape and size. If you put one <u>congruent</u> shape on top of the other, they would be exactly the same. In math, this is most often used to describe <u>congruent</u> triangles.

consecutive—*adj*. occurring in order, one right after the other. In math, it is most often used to describe <u>consecutive</u> numbers in a number pattern. Players also talk about how hard it is to play on <u>consecutive</u> days in sports like baseball and basketball because they don't get to rest between games.

convert—*v.* to change from one system of measurement to another. Most often used when <u>converting</u> our system of measurements to the metric system. See the metrics page at the end of this section for some common measurements and <u>conversions</u>.

converge—*v.* to come together at a point. Lines <u>converge</u>. So do rivers. In Pennsylvania, the Allegheny and Monongahela rivers <u>converge</u> to form the Ohio River.

coordinate plane—*n.* an *x-y* axis on which coordinate points can be plotted.

coordinates—*n.* a set of numbers that shows where a point goes on a coordinate plane.

data—*n.* facts and figures; the information you are given in a math problem. Test questions are always asking you to look at the <u>data</u> and answer the question.

denominator—*n.* the number under the line in a fraction.

diagonal—*n.* in a rectangle, a line slanting from one corner to the other. The "Diver Down" flag used by scuba divers has a diagonal line across it—that's a good way to get a visual of the word <u>diagonal</u>.

diameter—*n.* the length across the middle of a circle. If you are given the radius of the circle, double it to get the <u>diameter</u>: $d = 2r$

digit—*n.* 1, 2, 3, 4, 5, 6, 7, 8, 9, and 0 are digits. Math problems are always using two-<u>digit</u> numbers (also called tens: 23, 61), three-<u>digit</u> numbers (also called hundreds: 154, 982), and four-<u>digit</u> numbers (also called thousands:1,468).

dimensions—*n.* the length, width, and/or height of an object. Geometric shapes have <u>dimensions</u>, houses have <u>dimensions</u>, football fields have <u>dimensions</u>. Pretty much everything you can see has <u>dimensions</u>.

dividend—*n.* a number divided by another number. In the math problem 64 ÷ 6, 64 is the <u>dividend</u> (6 is the divisor).

divisor—*n.* the number that divides another number. See *dividend.*

domain—*n.* the set of the first coordinates of a group of ordered pairs. (The set of second coordinates is the *range.*) It also means

DOUBLE MEANING
convert—**v.**
to change from one religion or set of beliefs to another (social studies).

coordinate plane

diagonal

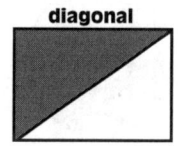

DOUBLE MEANING
domain—**n.**
territory ruled by a king or queen (social studies).

To remember equivalent, think of the word "equal."

"the territory ruled by a king or queen," so to remember it, you can think of it as a range of numbers under a king or queen's "domain."

equivalent—*adj.* the same; equal. Sometimes a math problem says "Find the answer that is <u>equivalent</u> to . . . whatever. " All that means is you find the answer that is the same or equal to . . . whatever.

estimate—*v.* to make a reasonable guess. When a math problem asks you to <u>estimate</u>, it means look at the data and make a guess that makes sense. I <u>estimate</u> things every day—from how long it's going to take to get ready for school to how much trouble I am going to get in for missing the bus because I <u>underestimated</u> how long it would take to get ready for school.

exponent—*n.* a number off to the upper right of another number that shows the power to which the number is raised. That means whatever the <u>exponent</u> is, you multiply a number times itself that many times. $4^3 = 4 \times 4 \times 4 = 64$.

factor—*n.* a number that can be multiplied with others to achieve a product. Hmm. How can I put this. Pick a number. The numbers you multiply to get that number are its <u>factors</u>. Take the number 27, for instance, some of its <u>factors</u> are 3 x 3 x 3 (= 27). Some others are 9 x 3 (= 27). Some others are 27 x 1 (= 27). The number 13 has <u>factors</u> of 13 x 1 (= 13). Note: 13 is also a prime number—which means its only <u>factors</u> are itself and 1.

graphs—*n.* you need to know how to read two main kinds of graphs—circle graphs and bar graphs. A <u>circle graph</u> is also called a pie graph. The different sized slices of pie show relative proportions of something, like the amount of attention four brothers and sisters get from their parents. A <u>bar graph</u> measures things on an *x*- and *y*-axis. The *x*-axis stands for one thing (like years) and the *y*-axis stands for another (like height). Note: You may also see <u>line graphs</u> here and there: they look like a jagged mountain top set on an *x*-axis.

horizontal—*adj.* straight across. To remember the word, think of a "horizon."

hypotenuse—*n.* the longest side of a right triangle; the side opposite the 90° angle. About the only time you will see questions about the <u>hypotenuse</u> is in questions about right triangles.

integer—*n.* positive whole numbers, negative whole numbers, and zero are <u>integers</u>. No fractions and no decimals are <u>integers</u>—ever! Think of <u>integers</u> as having too much "integrity" to get involved with messy fractions and decimals.

intersect—*v.* to cross each other. Lines <u>intersect</u> on graphs. To remember it, think of street <u>intersections</u>—where streets cross each other.

irrational number—*n.* a number that cannot be expressed as a fraction or decimal. Like π, or $\sqrt{2}$. You can put an <u>irrational num-</u>

Bar Graph

Circle Graph (Pie Graph)

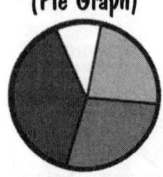

Circle the integers.

1/2
.6
6
–6
–2
0
3.2
6.9
3/4
17
–12
243

ber on a number line, but you can't express the number precisely, like you can with 1.5 and –3. (See the definition for *rational number* if you don't get it yet.)

lowest common denominator—*n.* the smallest whole number that can be divided evenly by the denominators of two fractions. For example, the lowest common denominator for 1/4 and 1/5 is 20. To add 1/4 + 1/5 you must convert them to 5/20 (from 1/4) and 4/20 (from 1/5).

mean—*n.* see the definition for *average*; they are the same thing.

median—*n.* in a group of numbers, it is the one in the middle. *Example*: Here is a group of numbers: 23, 26, 31, 56, 67, 78, 86, 102, 165, 234, 254. The median is 78—it is the middle number in this series.

mode—*n.* in a group of numbers, it is the number that occurs most often. *Example*: Here is a group of numbers: 23, 24, 24, 25, 26, 27, 28, 29, 29, 30, 31, 32, 32, 32, 33, 34. The mode is 32. It occurs three times—the most of any number in this series.

multiple—*n.* a number that you can divide another number into and get zero remainder. 4, 8, and 12 are multiples of 2.

negative number—*n.* a number less than zero. On a number line, the numbers to the left of 0 are negative numbers.

numerator—*n.* the number that is divided by the denominator.

odds—*n.* a ratio of favorable to unfavorable outcomes. For example, what are the odds Tim Duncan will hit a 20-foot jump shot if he makes four out of every nine 20-footers he takes? The odds are the number of successful attempts over the number of unsuccessful attempts. In this case, 4/5.

ordered pair—*n.* the actual coordinates on a coordinate plane (*x,y*). (See the definition for *coordinates*.)

order of operations—*n.* the sequence by which you do the operations in an equation. To remember the correct order of operations, think of PEMDAS ("Please Excuse My Dear Aunt Sally"). The order of operations is: parentheses, exponents, multiplication, division, addition, subtraction.

parallel—*adj.* relating to lines traveling alongside each other at the same distance without ever touching. Train tracks are parallel.

perimeter—*n.* the outside edge of an object or shape. Think about soldiers patrolling the perimeter of their outpost. That means they are patrolling the edges of their camp, making sure the enemy isn't planning any funny business.

perpendicular—*adj.* relating to lines meeting each other at a right (90⁰) angle. Perpendicular is kind of the opposite of *parallel*. They are mentioned in the same sentence—and the same math problem—all the time.

perspective—*n.* the appearance of depth or three dimensions; when you draw something on a piece of paper, but you give it three

To remember median, think of the "median" that separates one side of a highway from the other. It runs down the middle of the highway.

$$\frac{3}{5}$$

numerator
denominator

To remember order of operations, think about a surgeon who has to operate. First he has to clean up, then he has to put the patient under, then he makes his first incision. He always has an "order of operations."

perspective

dimensions, so it looks like real life. Think about drawing a road that recedes into the distance—the sides of the road get closer together as they go away into the distance. Oh heck, sometimes a picture is worth a thousand words, so just look at the picture of the road on the left. That's <u>perspective</u>.

point—*n.* in geometry, a spot marked in space. Basically, a <u>point</u> is used in questions about "the distance between two points" and "the straight line between points A and B." Stuff like that. The <u>points</u> are the dots.

polygon—*n.* a flat shape with three or more straight sides. A <u>polygon</u> is any shape with flat sides, really, from a triangle to a rectangle to an octagon to whatever a shape with 28 sides is called, and beyond . . . .

positive number—*n.* a number greater than zero. On a number line, the numbers to the right of 0 are <u>positive numbers</u>.

prime number—*n.* a positive whole number with only itself and one as factors. That means you can't divide any other number into it without getting a remainder. 17 is a <u>prime number</u>. 23 is a <u>prime number</u>. Try all night, you can't divide any other numbers into them without getting a remainder. (See the definition for <u>factor</u> in this section for more information.)

probability—*n.* the chance that something will happen, shown as a ratio of favorable outcomes to possible outcomes.

product—*n.* the answer to a multiplication problem. The <u>product</u> of 3 x 6 is 18.

proportion—*n.* a comparison of equivalent ratios. *Example*: 3/6 = 1/2 or 3:6 = 1:2.

Pythagorean theorem—*n.* for right triangles, the sum of the squares of a right triangle's sides is equal to the square of the hypotenuse. $a^2 + b^2 = \text{hyp}^2$. (See the definitions for *hypotenuse* and *triangles* in Math for more information.)

quadrilateral—*n.* a four-sided polygon. Squares, rectangles, and rhombuses are all <u>quadrilaterals</u>.

radius—*n.* the line from the center of a circle to its outside edge. The <u>radius</u> is half a circle's diameter.

random—*adj.* having no pattern or reason; out of the blue. Lottery numbers are picked at <u>random</u>.

rate—*n.* one thing measured in terms of another thing. Miles per hour. Words per minute. Gallons per flush. Inches per year. Those are all <u>rates</u>.

ratio—*n.* the relationship between two quantities. <u>Ratios</u> can be expressed as fractions (the <u>ratio</u> of four to nine is 4/9) or with a colon (the <u>ratio</u> of six to seven is 6:7).

rational number—*n.* a number that can be expressed as a ratio of two integers. 7 is a <u>rational number</u> (it can be expressed as 7/1). –2/3 is a <u>rational number</u>. 45.4 is a <u>rational number</u>.

Antonym

**negative number—
n. a number
less than zero. The
numbers to the
left of 0 on a
number line**

On the TAAS

**How would the
product 5 x 5 x 5
be expressed in
exponential
notation?**

Related Word

**random sample—n.
a group of
numbers or
values chosen
out of the blue.**

**DOUBLE MEANING
rate—v.
to judge;
to rank (social
studies).**

reflection—*n.* a shape that is flipped, so it's the same, but backwards. Think of it like your <u>reflection</u> in the mirror. All the sides are the same length and the angles are the same size; they are just positioned exactly opposite of where they were.

rotation—*n.* movement in a circular motion around a fixed point. When a geometric shape is <u>rotated</u>, its shape stays the same but the side that was on the bottom may now be on the top.

scale—*n.* when talking about models, scale is the relationship between the size of the model and the size of the real-life object. So if a <u>scale</u> model of an airplane is 1:8, that means the real airplane is eight times as big as the model.

scatterplot—*n.* a "graph" used to show the relationship between two or more variables. So if one class's math scores were on a <u>scatterplot</u>, and lots of students were getting Bs, it would look like this:

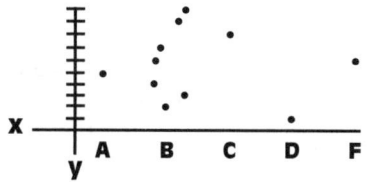

sequence—*n.* the order something happens in. In math, it usually means a number <u>sequence</u>, like 2,4,6,8 . . . or a <u>sequence</u> of operations, like performing operations inside parentheses first.

square—*n.* a polygon with four equal sides and four right angles.

square—*n.* the number you get when you multiply a number by itself. The square of 3 (3 x 3) is 9. The square of 11 (11 x 11) = 121.

square root—*n.* the divisor of a number that when squared gives that number. Signified by the $\sqrt{}$ sign, it means that if you square the number under the $\sqrt{}$, you get that number. (The *root* of the *square*—get it?)

sum—*n.* the answer to an addition problem. The <u>sum</u> of 4 + 5 is 9.

symmetry—*n.* when the stuff on one side of a dividing line matches the stuff on the other. If you draw a line down the middle of your face, the parts on the left match the parts on the right. Your face has <u>symmetry</u>. It is <u>symmetrical</u>. So are some shapes and some graphs.

terminate—*v.* to end; to stop. The word is used in math to describe where decimals <u>terminate</u>. Repeating decimals never <u>terminate</u>—they repeat forever. To remember it, think of the musclebound actor Arnold Schwarzenegger. He played a cyborg in the *Terminator*, and he "ended" any puny little people who got in his way.

three-dimensional—*adj.* having three dimensions, which gives an object depth. Any real object is <u>three-dimensional</u>. Also written as <u>3-D</u>.

Please square these numbers:
2
45
–3
–41
7
–6

Symmetry

triangle—*n.* a shape with three sides and three angles. There are four kinds of <u>triangles</u> you need to know:

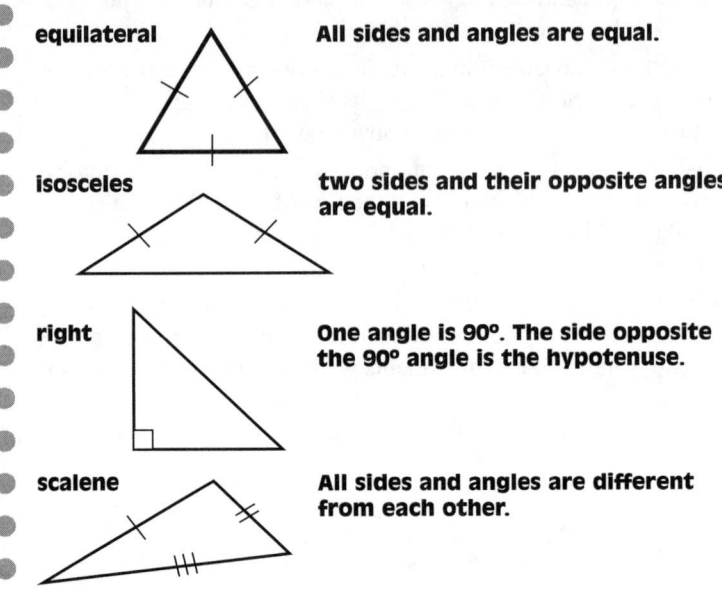

equilateral　　　　　　**All sides and angles are equal.**

isosceles　　　　　　**two sides and their opposite angles are equal.**

right　　　　　　**One angle is 90°. The side opposite the 90° angle is the hypotenuse.**

scalene　　　　　　**All sides and angles are different from each other.**

unit cost—*n.* the cost of each single thing. <u>Unit cost</u> is usually used in problems where you have to find out how much it costs to make something. For example: What is the unit cost of gum if you can make 50,000 pieces of gum for $725. Answer: $.0145 per piece of gum. (Divide $725 by 50,000). Then a problem might ask you to compare that <u>unit cost</u> to another one, so you can see which manufacturing method is cheaper! (Watch out! You are being trained.)

variable—*n.* a symbol whose value can change. In math, the <u>variable</u> is usually called x or y. That means you can plug in different numbers for the variable x or y or z or whatever. To remember the word, think of watching a weather report. The weatherman often says that "winds are <u>variable</u>," and weather itself is always variable (changing).

vertical—*adj.* going straight up and down. Like a flag pole.

volume—*n.* the amount of space something occupies. You can get Coca-Cola in all kinds of different <u>volumes</u>, from a 12-ounce can to a 16-ounce bottle to a three-liter bottle. I prefer the three-liter bottle.

whole number—*n.* an integer. Positive or negative. Not a fraction, not a decimal, not an irrational number. Just nice, clean integers are <u>whole numbers</u>.

Whiz Quiz

Solve the following problems with the variables $x=2$ and $y=3$

$2x$

$4y$

$-5y$

$x - y$

$2y + 7x$

$-2x - 4y$

Math
Measurements Page

METRIC AND
BRITISH IMPERIAL MEASUREMENTS

Measurement conversion charts are provided on most math tests, so it's important you know how to read them. Measuring is the only time I wish I was European. They have things so easy when it comes to measuring. As you probably know, their metric system is all based on tens. Anyway, here are the measurements that are used most often on tests—in metric and British Imperial (that's what we use). Don't ask me why we use British Imperial and the English use metrics. Because I don't know.

BRITISH IMPERIAL
Distance

Foot	12 inches
Yard	3 feet
Mile	1,760 yards

Volume

Pint	16 ounces
Quart	2 pints
Gallon	4 quarts

Weight

Pound	16 ounces
Ton	2,000 pounds

METRIC
Distance

Centimeter	10 millimeters
Meter	100 centimeters
Kilometer	1,000 meters

Volume

Liter	1,000 milliliters

Weight

Gram	1,000 milligrams
Kilogram	1,000 grams
Metric ton	1,000 kilograms

COMMON CONVERSIONS
(ALL CONVERSIONS ARE APPROXIMATE)
Distance

BRITISH IMPERIAL	METRIC
Inch	about 3 centimeters
Yard	about 1 meter
Mile	about 1.6 kilometers

Volume

BRITISH IMPERIAL	METRIC
Ounce	about 29 milliliters
Cup	about 1/4 liter
Gallon	about 3.79 liters

Weight

BRITISH IMPERIAL	METRIC
Ounce	about 29 grams
Pound	about 450 grams
	(about 1/2 kilogram)

WhizWords

coordinate plane,
coordinates
graphs (bar, circle,
and line)

Math

Graphs

So many people say—why do I need to learn all this math? I will never use it in my real life. I think I'll spend my time doing important things, like shopping on eBay.

Well, nothing could be further from the truth. Lots of people use math every day. In baseball, they use math to calculate hitters' batting averages. Players can then use those batting averages to negotiate their salaries. Then, when they are buying their yachts and mansions, they use math to calculate sales tax and change. Even if you're not an All-Star baseball player, you'll still need to know math. How else are you going to budget to save up for those great deals on eBay?

Now that you are convinced, let's start with something relatively simple that is used all the time: a graph. There is nothing better for explaining things in an easy-to-read format than a **coordinate plane** and a **graph**.

USING MATH TO EXPLAIN YOUR LIFE EXERCISE

You can use a graph to represent just about any relationship. I have created the following graphs that represent:

**My math test grades last semester
67, 92, 89, 94, 78, 81, 88, 97**

The four TV shows I watch the most, in relative proportion to the amount of time spent viewing:

Digimon 10%
Moesha 30%
Buffy 20%
Baseball 40%

My height over the years:

Years	3	6	9	12
Feet	3	3.5	4	4.75

Draw the same three graphs for your most recent math grades, viewing time for your favorite TV shows, and your height at different ages. Try to think of three more things you can represent on a graph. Here are some ideas: raises or drops in your allowance in the last two years (bar); the proportions of kinds of food you eat every day (circle), and the amount of time you spend daily on various activities like sleeping, eating, going to school, doing homework, and e-mailing your friends.

Math

Circles

So you need more proof that math is all around you? Fine. Let's talk about circles. Circles are obviously everywhere, from the portholes on a ship to the circles under your parents' eyes. The invention of the wheel, the hardest working circle of all time, was a big event, right up there with the invention of Pop Rocks and Napster.

Of course on math tests, you have to do a little more than just appreciate the importance of roundness. You have to be able to calculate **diameters** and **circumferences** of circles of all sizes.

DIFFERENT SIZE CIRCLES EXERCISE

I have given you a variety of circles below. I want you to find the circumference and diameter of each. I'm even going to help you out a bit. Here are the equations for each:

Diameter = 2r

Circumference = 2πr

Note: Circles not drawn to scale.

Now, get a ruler. Go and find five more circles in your house and measure the radius—that's half the diameter. Use those measurements to find the diameter and the circumference of the circles you found. Don't know where to start? Try the kitchen, the home of circular housewares.

Note: π is the ratio of the circumference of a circle to its diameter. The actual value for π is approximately 3.14159.

WhizWords

integer
irrational number
negative number
positive number
prime number
rational number
whole number

Math

Number Types

Still not convinced of math's importance in your everyday existence? I was like you once, before I saw the light. One part of math you can't dispute is that numbers are everywhere. We measure ingredients, tell time, and count the days until summer vacation.

What you probably don't do while you are counting the days to summer vacation is think about what kind of number you have in your head. The "31" in "31 days until summer vacation" is an **integer**, a **positive number**, a **prime number**, a **rational number**, and a **whole number**. Those are the kinds of things you need to know for the TAAS and other tests. So let's review.

NUMBERS YOU SEE EVERY DAY EXERCISE

Label each of the numbers with all of the number types from above that match. If none match, write "none." I'll do the first couple so you get the idea.

17 years old integer, positive number, prime number, rational number, whole number

–3 degrees integer, negative number, rational number, whole number

$.79 Snickers bar _____
_____

.327 batting average _____
_____

2 1/2 weeks _____
_____

4 hours _____
_____

–12 under par _____
_____

a drink coaster with a circumference _____
of 6π (okay, I'm stretching here) _____

WhizWords
average
mean
median
mode

Math
Number Relationships

Whether you believe that math affects your everyday life or not, you still have to take tests about it. One thing that shows up on all sorts of math tests, including the TAAS, is number relationships. Questions about number relationships usually involve long lists of numbers and ask you to figure out the **mean**, **median** or **mode**. Sometimes all three.

Just remember:
- **mean** (means average)
- **median** (in the middle of the road)
- **mode** (sounds like most)

So let's get to it.

TEST GRADES EXERCISE
Find the mean, median, and mode of my grades last year on tests in English language arts, math, science, and Social Studies.

		Mean	Median	Mode
English	56, 92, 87, 79, 95, 92, 99			
Math	78, 82, 91, 79, 78, 97, 93			
Science	94, 91, 99, 100, 89, 94, 94			
Social Studies	102, 84, 72, 67, 84, 94, 84			

Find the mean, median, and mode of these three baseball players' batting averages over their careers.

		Mean	Median	Mode
Paul O'Neill	.333, .256, .252, .276, .270, .256, .246, .311, .359, .300, .302, .324, .317, .285, .283			
Manny Ramirez	.269, .308, .309, .328, .294, .333, .351			
Alex Rodriguez	.232, .358, .300, .310, .285, .316			
Derek Jeter	.314, .291, .324, .349, .339			
Tony Gwynn	.289, .309, .351, .317, .329, .370, .313, .336, .309, .317, .317, .358, .394, .368, .353, .372, .321, .338, .323			

WhizTip

For more practice, line up your grades from last semester or last year and find the mean, median, and mode.

Chapter 4

Science

absorb—*v.* to soak up. Commercials for paper towels brag about how they <u>absorb</u> spills. You have probably heard your teacher say that she hopes you are <u>absorbing</u> everything she says.

acclimatization—*n.* adaptation to changes in climates. It took a while for the <u>acclimatization</u> of my new pet snake to its new aquarium. It didn't eat for a week!

adhere—*v.* to stick to. Scotch tape <u>adheres</u> to paper quite well. It does not <u>adhere</u> to running water.

alloy—*n.* a metal made by melting different metals together. Bronze is an <u>alloy</u> of copper and tin.

artery—*n.* a blood vessel carrying blood from the heart.

asteroids—*n.* a bunch of big rocks orbiting the sun, kind of like mini-planets. Most <u>asteroids</u> are in between the planets Mars and Jupiter. In sci-fi movies, space ships are always getting caught up in <u>asteroid</u> belts. Just remember, they are called "belts" because they are "wrapping around" the sun.

atmosphere—*n.* the layer of gases surrounding the Earth or another planet. The Earth's <u>atmosphere</u> is mostly oxygen and nitrogen.

atom—*n.* the smallest unit of an element that has all the properties of that element. Everything in the world is made up of <u>atoms</u>. The <u>atom</u> bomb gets its power from when <u>atoms</u> are split—that's how much energy is stored up in this tiny little particle. It's kind of scary when you think about it.

axis—*n.* the center around which something rotates. <u>Axis</u> is usually used when talking about a planet (like the Earth) rotating on its <u>axis</u>.

bacteria—*n.* one-celled organisms. They are all around us, but you can't see them. My mom buys anti-<u>bacterial</u> soap because she thinks me and my sister are getting too many colds—she thinks it's because of all the <u>bacteria</u> on our hands.

beneficial—*adj.* helpful; good. Learning the words in this book should prove to be <u>beneficial</u> to your grades. Hey, it can't hurt!

biomass—*n.* all of the living things in an environment. The *mass* of *bio*—get it?

buoyant—*adj.* it floats! Ivory soap is <u>buoyant</u>, but Zest and Irish Spring sink like stones.

capillary—*n.* an itty bitty blood vessel that attaches small veins to small arteries. If you are looking at a road map, the superhighways are major veins and arteries, the state highways are smaller veins and arteries, and the little roads and streets connecting the state highways are <u>capillaries</u>.

carbohydrate—*n.* a compound composed of carbon, hydrogen, and oxygen. (In foods we eat, most of the carbohydrates are found in sugar and starch.) The night before a baseball game I load up on <u>carbohydrates</u> by eating spaghetti for dinner and two bananas for dessert. For some reason, I never sleep very well.

carbon—*n.* the element found in all living things. One of the ways scientists find the age of a fossil is to use <u>carbon</u> dating. That's when they measure how much <u>carbon</u> is left in a fossil and calculate how old that makes it.

catalyst—*n.* in science, a substance that speeds up a chemical reaction. Fire is a <u>catalyst</u> for turning water into evaporated water.

catastrophic—*adj.* tragic and awful, causing great pain and suffering. I hope Alex Rodriguez doesn't suffer a <u>catastrophic</u> injury to his knee. That would ruin the Rangers' season.

categorize—*v.* to divide up into groups. When my dad does the laundry, he always <u>categorizes</u> the clothes as whites and colors. I, on the other hand, just throw everything in together.

celestial—*adj.* related to the stars and the universe. Planets and asteroids and suns and stuff are all called "<u>celestial</u> bodies."

cell—*n.* the smallest, most basic part of a plant or animal. A <u>cell</u> is filled with protoplasm, has a nucleus near its center, and has a membrane that keeps it all together.

centrifugal force—*n.* moving away from the center. When you swing a bucket of water around in a circle real fast, and the water doesn't fall out, that's <u>centrifugal force</u>!

chain reaction—*n.* a series of events in which one thing leads to another, which leads to another. I saw a <u>chain reaction</u> accident on the highway once when a semi jackknifed, and all of the cars behind it ran into each other.

chemical energy—*n.* the energy released in a chemical reaction. Energy is usually released as heat, so think of reactions where heat is released.

DOUBLE MEANING
catalyst—n. someone who makes things happen. Usually used in social studies when talking about a movement or revolution. The feminist movement's leader, Gloria Steinem, was a catalyst for change for women in the 1960s.

Antonym
centripetal force—n. Moving toward a center. It's what keeps the planets orbiting around the sun.

chloroplast—*n*. the part of a plant cell that contains the chlorophyll.

circulatory system—*n*. the organs that move blood around the body, including the heart, veins, arteries, and capillaries. Just think of the pipes and plumbing that circulate water in your house. They are your house's circulatory system.

collision—*n*. the slamming of one thing into another. When there is a collision between an opponent's bat and my best pitch, that is not good.

complement—*v*. to make complete. In science, the word is often used to describe how an organ's structure complements its function. The shape of your esophagus (throat) complements its function by being straight and slippery—so food slides down it easily.

component—*n*. a part of a system or machine. The components of my stereo are the receiver, the CD player, and the five-speaker surround sound system.

compost—*n*. decayed organic matter that is used as fertilizer. Compost is made of a mixture of dead plants, and maybe manure. It smells awful, but it makes my mom's tomatoes grow fast.

compound—*n*. in chemistry, the new substance formed when one or more elements are added together. Water is a compound made of one hydrogen and two oxygen atoms.

condensation point—*n*. the temperature at which a gas condenses into a liquid. Clouds formed over the Rangers' last home game when the air temperature reached the condensation point. Clouds form when liquid collects on dust particles in the air.

conductor—*n*. a material that takes an electric current from one point to another. Copper wire is a good conductor. So are you, so stay away from electricity!

conservation—*n*. the protection of natural resources. Conservation is important if we are to keep the few natural wonders this country has left, like the Grand Canyon and Yellowstone National Park.

consistency—*n*. the degree of firmness or viscosity of a substance. A tub of margarine has a consistency similar to soft ice cream. The consistency of motor oil depends on the temperature—it gets really thick and gooey as the temperature drops.

contaminate—*v*. to make impure. Lots of things we do every day contaminate the environment. Driving a car contaminates the environment with carbon monoxide and other gases. Eating fast food contaminates the environment with all of the packaging it comes in, not to mention the pollution from the factories that make the packaging. It's almost like if you don't live in an underground house fueled by solar panels and windmills, you are contaminating the environment! About all we can do is try to reduce the amount of contaminants we produce, but we can never eliminate them.

continental drift—*n*. the theory that the continents are always drifting—they are not fixed. The continents drift only an inch or so each year, but over millions and billions of years, those inches turn

DOUBLE MEANING

compound word— **n.** a word made of two words, like "groundwater" (ground + water = groundwater) (English language arts).

Think of a train conductor getting you from one point to the next.

DOUBLE MEANING

consistency—**n.** the ability to be counted on to behave the same way or produce the same thing all the time.

into thousands of miles.

current—*n.* the flow of electricity.

cyclical—*adj.* happening in cycles. In chemistry, the word <u>cyclical</u> has to do with chemical compounds that have atoms arranged in a closed chain. In real life, lots of things are <u>cyclical</u>. The changing of seasons is the most obvious.

cytoplasm—*n.* the protoplasm outside the cell's nucleus.

decay—*v.* to rot; to break down. When you die, unless you have yourself cryogenically frozen or you are cremated, your body will <u>decay</u>. I plan on going the cryogenically frozen route, like in the original *Austin Powers* movie. Groovy baby, yeah!

decompose—*v.* to rot; to break down. See *decay* above.

dehydrate—*v.* to remove the water from. <u>Dehydrated</u> food like beef jerky has had the water taken out—that's why it's all shriveled. A few games ago I got <u>dehydrated</u> and started feeling dizzy because I didn't drink enough water and it was 98 degrees out.

density—*n.* the amount of something per unit measure. Just remember, light things are usually less <u>dense</u> than heavy things.

deteriorate—*v.* to get worse. When you hear someone say "his health is <u>deteriorating</u>," that means it is getting worse. When you hear someone say "that house is <u>deteriorating</u>" that means it is falling apart because no one is keeping it up.

digestive system—*n.* the parts of your body that work together to break down food so it can be converted into energy. Your <u>digestive system</u> is made up of the alimentary canal, which is basically every part of your body the food touches, from your mouth all the way down to . . . well, you know.

dilate—*v.* to get wide. Your pupils <u>dilate</u> when there isn't much light. That's because when they are wider, they can let more light in.

dissolve—*v.* to mix with a liquid. Kool Aid <u>dissolves</u> in water to make a tasty, refreshing drink.

distill—*v.* to purify by evaporation and then condensation. <u>Distilled</u> water has had all of the impurities boiled out. What they do is boil the water and then capture the steam—that steam doesn't have any of the impurities that were in the water. They then drop the temperature on the steam and—ta da!—<u>distilled</u> water.

dominant trait—*n.* when paired with a recessive trait, this is the trait that "wins"—the <u>dominant</u> trait beats the recessive trait. So if the <u>dominant</u> trait in a species of butterfly is big wings and the recessive trait is little wings, a butterfly that has one gene for each will have "big wings."

dormant—*adj.* sleeping; inactive. Lots of animals, insects, and plants go <u>dormant</u> over the winter, sleeping until spring. When the Texas Rangers' bats go <u>dormant</u>, that means no one is getting any hits, and the team is doomed.

eclipse—*v.* to block the light. When the moon <u>eclipses</u> the sun, it's always a big deal. It's all over the news, people are making special <u>eclipse</u> viewers out of paper and cardboard boxes. It's bigger than

DOUBLE MEANING
**current—n.
the continuous
movement of
water (science).**

**Whenever you
see a word with
"plasm" in it,
you know it has
something to
do with cells.**

WhizTip

**I have found that
when I don't read
regularly, my
vocabulary starts
to deteriorate.**

Science

Name five organisms that are part of an ecosystem at or near your home.

1. _____
2. _____
3. _____
4. _____
5. _____

Groundhog Day! As you have probably heard a million times, never look at an <u>eclipse</u>. It could make you go blind.

ecosystem—*n.* the combination of organisms and the place they live. My backyard is an <u>ecosystem</u> all by itself. It's got my dad's Koi pond filled with goldfish and frogs, my mom's tomato patch, and all of the bugs and other animals that call my backyard home. There are probably hundreds of species of plants and animals making up the <u>ecosystem</u> back there.

efficient—*adj.* not wasting time or energy. I have often found that I study most <u>efficiently</u> when there is no noise. If I turn on the radio or TV, it takes me forever to get anything done.

electron—*n.* a tiny particle in an atom's nucleus that has a negative charge. There are the same number of protons (+) and <u>electrons</u> (−) in an atom's nucleus. Their opposite charges cancel each other out.

element—*n.* a substance that has only one kind of atom. There are 118 <u>elements</u>. My favorite is helium, because it's the <u>element</u> that makes your voice high and squeaky.

endocrine system—*n.* the body's endocrine glands, ductless organs that secrete hormones directly into the blood. The <u>endocrine system</u> includes the thyroid, pituitary, and adrenal glands, plus a bunch more I don't have room to list here. (See the Science exercises that follow for all of the components.)

endothermic—*adj.* absorbing heat. Think of <u>indoors</u> for <u>endothermic</u> reactions. It's a reaction that brings heat "inside."

entropy—*n.* disorder or chaos in a system. So if the Texas Rangers have three injured players, they have <u>entropy</u> on the team—disorder and chaos.

epicenter—*n.* the location directly over the center of an earthquake. You hear the word on the nightly news all the time when they are talking about earthquakes, like "The <u>epicenter</u> of the earthquake is located 150 miles west of San Diego, right here where I am standing! Aaaaaaahhhgggggghhh!" And then the camera fritzes off.

equilibrium—*n.* a condition in which all forces cancel each other out, resulting in balance. Remember it by thinking of the word "equal." <u>Equilibrium</u> happens when opposing forces are <u>equal</u>.

erosion—*n.* the process of soil being worn away, usually by water and wind. A huge windstorm in West Texas caused a lot of <u>erosion</u>—all the topsoil was basically blown over to East Texas.

eruption—*n.* the explosion of a volcano. The <u>eruption</u> of Mount Vesuvius in A.D. 79 ended up burying two entire cities in lava and ash. They have only recently started excavating the site.

ethics—*n.* rules that govern a profession. Medical <u>ethics</u> start with the promise that doctors "First, do no harm." That means the most important thing for a doctor is not to make you any sicker than you already are.

evaluate—*v.* to study so you can form an opinion. After <u>evaluating</u> the situation, I decided that trying to jump the 27-foot-wide creek on my mountain bike would be insane.

evaporation—*n.* the process of a liquid turning into a gas. I left a

Antonym

exothermic—adj. releasing heat. Think of an EXIT sign for exothermic reactions.

Do an Internet search and find the most recent volcano eruption in the United States.

glass of Kool Aid on my bedroom window sill and forgot about it. A few weeks later, all the liquid had <u>evaporated</u>, and all that was left was red, crusty goo. (Also see the definitions in this section for *distill* and *condensation point*.)

evolve—*v.* to change for the better. The theory of evolution is based on the idea that animals <u>evolve</u> to better take advantage of their environment. So if the environment is full of scary, spike-headed monsters, it would be good for a species to <u>evolve</u> in ways that would protect it from the monsters. (Thick skins and fast legs come to mind.)

exothermic—*adj.* releasing heat. An <u>exothermic</u> reaction happens when substances react strongly to each other. For example, if you mix two substances in a test tube and the tube gets hot, that's an <u>exothermic</u> reaction. Heat has been released. (See *endothermic* for more on this.)

extinct—*adj.* no longer in existence. The dodo bird is <u>extinct</u>—there aren't any of them on the planet any more. Dinosaurs are <u>extinct</u>. My mom says real gentlemen are <u>extinct</u>. (I'm not sure what that means.)

extrapolate—*v.* to take things you know and make assumptions based on those things. If you have gotten As on all your science tests so far, you can <u>extrapolate</u> that you will get good grades on the rest of your science tests, too.

extraterrestrial—*adj.* outside the Earth. Lots of people think there are <u>extraterrestrial</u> beings in outer space. I think they're nuts.

fault—*n.* a break in a rock formation. Earthquakes happen along geologic <u>faults</u>, where a rock formation is broken and two big slabs of rock are rubbing against each other.

fertilize—*v.* to make fruitful or productive. When an animal's egg is <u>fertilized</u>, its offspring begins to grow. When crops are fertilized, they usually produce more fruits or vegetables.

food chain—*n.* a line of organisms that eat each other.

Name three more extinct animals or species.

1. _____
2. _____
3. _____

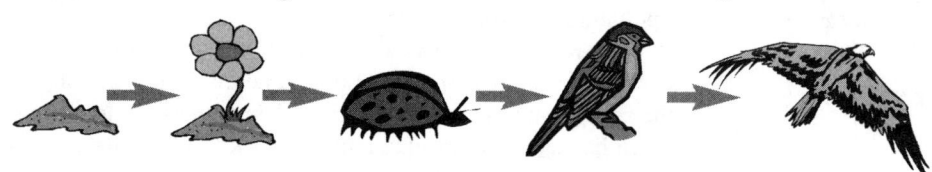

The <u>food chain</u> ends when an animal has no known predator—that means no other animals eat it. (Most hawks have nothing to fear.)

fossil fuel—*n.* fuel made from decayed organisms. Coal and oil are actually dead plants and animals that have decayed and have been compressed over millions of years into <u>fossil fuels</u>. Wind is not a <u>fossil fuel</u>. Neither is solar energy. They are renewable resources. (See the definition for *renewable*.)

friction—*n.* rough rubbing. The <u>friction</u> between two rock formations is what causes earthquakes.

fusion—*n.* in physics, a reaction in which atoms join together. In chemistry, when two substances are melted and mixed together. Basically, <u>fusion</u> takes place when two separate things combine into one thing.

Science

WhizTip

To remember galaxy, think of the first *Star Wars* movie that starts out with the words "In a galaxy far far away . . . ."

WhizQuiz

Think of a name for your generation that is better than Generation I.

WhizFact

The United Nations did an environmental study that concluded that the greenhouse effect is going to raise the temperature two to four degrees in the next 100 years.

DOUBLE MEANING

hemisphere—n. also stands for one-half of the brain—the left and right hemispheres.

galaxy—*n.* a big group of stars. The Earth and the sun and all of our sun's other planets are part of the Milky Way galaxy.

gene—*n.* a section of a chromosome that controls how part of an organism turns out. You have genes that control your eye color, your height, your looks—everything. And we are learning more and more about genes every day. Scientists just completed charting every gene—it was called the Human Genome Project.

generation—*n.* a group of people born around the same time; a stage in a succession. I have heard people calling our generation "Generation I" because we are the first to grow up with computers and the Internet.

genetics—*n.* the study of genes and heredity. The field of genetics is really booming right now. All of the stuff they are finding out about genes and how they affect our health and everything about us is really cool. Some people even think genetics will be the key to curing cancer!

geology—*n.* the study of rocks and the Earth. If I don't make it as a Major League pitcher, I think I'm going to be a geologist. I am almost as interested in earthquakes and volcanoes as I am in sports.

glaciation—*n.* the process of being overtaken by glaciers. Right now glaciation is in retreat. Instead of glaciers covering more of the Earth, they are melting. The Ice Age was a time of incredible glaciation.

greenhouse effect—*n.* the result of too many pollutants in the atmosphere; they let the sunlight in, but they don't let the heat back out. That causes the atmosphere to act like a greenhouse—keeping the heat in. Some people think the greenhouse effect is causing all the glaciers to melt around the polar icecaps.

groundwater—*n.* the water underneath the soil. Lots of people are afraid things like garbage dumps, strip mines, and nuclear waste sites are polluting the groundwater.

habitat—*n.* the normal environment where an organism lives. A water turtle's natural habitat is a pond. A hermit crab's natural habitat is the ocean. That's why when we have them as pets, we try to re-create their habitat inside an aquarium with rocks, sand, water, and some driftwood to climb on.

hemisphere—*n.* in earth sciences, the northern or southern half of the Earth. The equator is what separates the northern and southern hemispheres. To remember it, think hemisphere = half-a-sphere.

herbivore—*n.* an animal that eats plants. Cows are herbivores. Horses are herbivores. Vegetarians are herbivores. They all eat veggies, no meats.

hybrid—*n.* the offspring you get when you breed two different kinds of parents. You most often hear the word hybrid when people are talking about plants, like a corn hybrid that fends off insects or a hybrid tomato that is bigger and juicier than any other kind of tomato ever.

hydroelectric—*adj.* relating to electricity generated by water turning a turbine. My aunt in New York works at a public radio station that is run on hydroelectric power! All their power comes from a dam in a river outside the station.

hypothesis—*n*. a proposed explanation. Scientific progress is based on proving or disproving a <u>hypothesis</u>. If your <u>hypothesis</u> is "plants are mean," and you do an experiment that proves plants are mean, then your hypothesis is correct. If the experiment does not prove plants are mean, that DOES NOT mean the <u>hypothesis</u> is incorrect, only that your experiment didn't prove it.

igneous rock—*n*. rock that is formed from molten lava. It's not metamorphic, it's not sedimentary—it's igneous! (See the definition for *rock cycle*.)

ignite—*v*. to light on fire. When you <u>ignite</u> your Bunsen burner in science class, it gives off a blue flame.

immune—*adj*. being resistant to something bad. Lots of time you hear this word when people are talking about AIDS. AIDS is a disease that attacks your <u>immune</u> system, and makes it so you can't fight off any bacteria or other bad germs.

incinerate—*v*. to burn until there is nothing left but ashes. If you flew a space shuttle toward the sun, the sun's heat would <u>incinerate</u> it.

inertia—*n*. resistance to motion. My dad has a lot of <u>inertia</u> on weekends. It's hard to get him off the couch.

inexhaustible—*adj*. never-ending. It may seem like the Earth has an <u>inexhaustible</u> supply of oil and coal, but that's not true. If we keep going the way we are going now, we will be out of oil and coal in just a few hundred years. Then what?

insulation—*n*. protective material. There are lots of different kinds of <u>insulation</u> in your house. Heat <u>insulation</u> keeps heat from escaping your house. Water pipe <u>insulation</u> keeps them from freezing when it's cold. There is also <u>insulation</u> around electrical wires that keeps the wires from shocking everything they touch!

interact—*v*. to be involved with something else. Science is always testing how different things <u>interact</u>. It can be chemicals that <u>interact</u> with each other in an experiment; it can be animals <u>interacting</u> with each other in a habitat; it can be how the orbits of planets <u>interact</u> with each other.

interdependent—*adj*. relating to two things that rely on each other; mutual dependence. All habitats and ecosystems survive because the organisms in them are <u>interdependent</u>. One example of <u>interdependence</u> is flowers needing bees for pollination and bees needing flowers for their nectar.

intestine—*n*. one of two long tubes in your gut where food is digested. The small <u>intestine</u> measures about 22 feet long, and the large <u>intestine</u> measures about five feet long.

ion—*n*. an atom or molecule that used to be electrically neutral, but now it is either positive or negative because it gained or lost electrons. In other words, it used to be neutral (same number of protons and electrons) but it has since gained or lost an electron, so it is a positive <u>ion</u> (lost electrons) or negative <u>ion</u> (gained electrons).

kinetic—*adj*. having to do with movement. Most often, it is used to describe <u>kinetic</u> energy. To remember <u>kinetic</u>, think of calis-

WhizFact

There is a big debate about what to do with the dams in the West that produce hydroelectric power. Some want to destroy them and restore the rivers— and the fish.

WhizQuiz

Identify the rock's type:

basalt
_____
granite
_____
limestone
_____
marble

WhizQuiz

What's another kind of insulation? Try to think of one.

WhizQuiz

Which is longer?

100 feet of string or your small intestine

2,000 miles of highway or your small intestine

350-meter running track or your small intestine

Six yards of fabric or your small intestine

Science

thenics. They kind of sound the same, and they both have to do with movement.

land subsidence—*n.* the sinking of land. In some arid regions of the Southwest, tapping the water in the water table has resulted in <u>land subsidence</u>. As water is sucked out, the land sinks!

WhizQuiz

List three things that are lethal to humans:

1. _____
2. _____
3. _____

lethal—*adj.* causing death. Some states with capital punishment, like Texas, use a <u>lethal</u> injection to kill the prisoners on death row.

light year—*n.* the distance light travels in one year (9.46×10^{12} kilometers). It's important to remember that a <u>light year</u> is a measure of distance, not time.

lunar—*adj.* having to do with the moon. A <u>lunar</u> eclipse is when the Earth blocks the sun's light to the moon. The <u>lunar</u> module is a spaceship that landed on the moon.

magma—*n.* the molten rock below the Earth's surface, waiting to spew out in a volcano and then form igneous rock when it cools. I went on a vacation to Hawaii and I actually saw red, glowing <u>magma</u> where there are active volcanoes.

magnitude—*n.* a measure of the amount of energy an earthquake releases. Earthquakes' <u>magnitudes</u> are always measured. Small earthquakes have <u>magnitudes</u> from 2–3. Medium-size earthquakes have <u>magnitudes</u> from 4–6. Large earthquakes have <u>magnitudes</u> from 7–10.

mantle—*n.* the layer of rock between the Earth's crust and its core. So, we walk all over the crust, the core is boiling molten rock, and the only thing keeping the molten rock from us crust-dwellers is the <u>mantle</u>. Thank you, <u>mantle</u>!

meiosis—*n.* cell division in sexually reproducing organisms that produces a cell with half the required number of chromosomes that will then link up with the other half of the chromosomes from the other sex partner. Humans have 46 chromosomes—23 from each parent. <u>Meiosis</u> is what produces one of those 23-chromosome sex cells (called gametes).

membrane—*n.* as in cell membrane, the outer layer of the cell. The <u>membrane</u> keeps all the stuff inside the cell from floating out AND it keeps out the stuff the cell doesn't need.

metabolism—*n.* the chemical and physical changes that take place in cells; the changes that take place in the body. You have probably heard people say "I have a high <u>metabolism</u>—I eat anything I want all day and I don't gain a pound." Someone with a high <u>metabolism</u> has a body that is working really fast and efficiently to burn up all the food it gets.

Related Word

metamorphosis—n. the change from one thing to another.

metamorphic rock—*n.* rock that was changed from one kind of rock to another by pressure or temperature. It's not sedimentary, it's not igneous—it's <u>metamorphic</u>! (See the definition for *rock cycle*.)

meteor—*n.* the trail behind a meteorite caused by the meteorite entering the Earth's atmosphere. Last year I saw the most awesome <u>meteor</u> shower I have ever seen. It was like the sky was on fire—there were so many <u>meteors</u> burning up as they entered our atmosphere.

mineral—*n.* a natural substance with a definite chemical and crystalline composition. A diamond is a <u>mineral</u>. So are gold and silver.

mitochondrion—*n.* the part of the cell that converts food into energy the body can use. It's at the last stage of digestion, working to turn that burger and fries into energy for your body.

mitosis—*n.* the division of a cell into two identical cells; the differentiation and segregation of replicated chromosomes in a cell's nucleus.

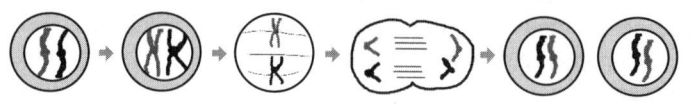

molecule—*n.* the smallest unit of a compound or an element. A <u>molecule</u> of water has two hydrogens and one oxygen atom—H_2O.

molten—*adj.* melted or liquefied by intense heat. The lava that comes out of volcanoes is <u>molten</u> rock.

mutation—*n.* a change in the genes of an organism from one generation to the next. The theory of evolution states that a <u>mutation</u> that helps an organism survive better than others will be passed down from generation to generation, because that organism and its offspring will have a better chance of living and having kids. That's why giraffes have long necks. They lived in a place where the food was up high, so the ones with the genetic <u>mutation</u> that gave them longer necks did better and had kids, while the ones with shorter necks couldn't get to the food, and died.

natural selection—*n.* the theory that organisms best suited for their environment survive and have offspring, and those who are not die and do not have offspring. Also known as "survival of the fittest." Kind of harsh, I know. But it is the way things work in nature. (See *mutation* for more on this.)

neutron—*n.* a particle that's in the nucleus of all atoms (except hydrogen.) A <u>neutron</u> has the same mass as a proton, but no electrical charge (it is neutral). So the nucleus of atoms has protons, electrons, and <u>neutrons</u> (except hydrogen).

nuclear energy—*n.* the energy released by a nuclear reaction. <u>Nuclear energy</u> makes up a big part of this country's energy production, but not nearly as much as energy produced by burning oil, coal, and natural gas. The thing is, <u>nuclear energy</u> plants can be much more dangerous than other energy sources. If something goes wrong and radiation escapes from <u>nuclear power</u> plant, people can get sick and die.

nucleus—*n.* 1) in a cell, the center of a cell containing the genes.

Related Word

meteorite—n. a space rock that enters the Earth's atmosphere and makes a meteor.

Related Word

magma (See its definition.)

WhizQuiz

Name a genetic mutation that helped this species survive:
Giraffe
Human
Elephant
Cheetah

WhizFact

Famous dangerous nuclear accidents:

Three-Mile Island, 1979 Pennsylvania, USA

Chernobyl, 1986 Chernobyl, Ukraine

The <u>nucleus</u> of a cell contains the parts that control the cell, like the <u>nucleus</u> of a baseball team is made up of the players that control whether a team wins or loses. 2) In an atom, the center of the atom containing protons, electrons, and neutrons.

nutrients—*n.* the stuff that nourishes your body. You see the word all the time on vitamin commercials—"VitaMight contains 127 essential <u>nutrients</u> to keep your body glowing like a lightbulb!" The fact is you get plenty of <u>nutrients</u> from the foods you eat, as long as you eat the right foods.

omnivore—*n.* an organism that eats all kinds of food, including plants and animals. Humans are <u>omnivores</u>. So are dogs.

orbit—*n.* the path of one celestial body around another. Planets occupy different <u>orbits</u> around the sun.

organic—*adj.* having to do with living organisms. When you see food labeled "organic" in the grocery store, that means it was grown with all <u>organic</u> materials—no chemicals or man-made substances were used.

organism—*n.* a living plant, animal, bacterium, protist, or fungus. I have used the word <u>organism</u> in tons of these science definitions. It's obviously because lots of science is concerned with the study of <u>organisms</u> and all of the things that affect <u>organisms</u>.

origin—*n.* the beginning. People are still debating on what the <u>origin</u> of life is. Some people say the <u>origin</u> of life is the Big Bang. Some people say God is the <u>origin</u> of all life. Other people think space aliens came here and planted the first living things. Others think the first living things came in on a meteorite from far, far away.

What is your town of origin?

oxidation—*n.* a reaction in which the atoms in an element lose electrons. The most common example of <u>oxidation</u> is the formation of rust. Metal atoms <u>oxidize</u>—they lose electrons—and rust forms.

ozone layer—*n.* a layer of our atmosphere that protects us from harmful sun rays. Pollution is causing holes in the <u>ozone layer</u>, which means those bad sun rays are making it all the way down to the Earth, where they can cause skin cancer. My mom always makes me wear sunscreen when I play baseball because she's worried about the holes in the <u>ozone layer</u>.

paleontologist—*n.* someone who studies fossils. If I don't become a baseball pitcher or a geologist, <u>paleontologist</u> is my third choice. Once, when I was fishing, I found a really cool fossil of a prehistoric fern that was imprinted on a piece of slate. I put it in a glass case and hung it on a wall in my room.

periodic table—*n.* the chart that lists all of the elements and their atomic numbers.

5 B	6 C	7 N	8 O
13 Al	14 Si	15 P	16 S
31 Ga	32 Ge	33 As	34 Se

pH—*n.* a measure of how acidic or alkaline a substance is.

photosynthesis—*n.* the process plants use to turn sunlight into energy. If people could perform <u>photosynthesis</u>, we wouldn't need to eat so much! We could just sit in the sun and get all the energy we need. Instead we have to cover ourselves in sunscreen and stay in the shade. Lucky plants!

precipitation—*n.* rain, snow, sleet, and hail. The weatherman said the odds of <u>precipitation</u> tomorrow are 50 percent. But he's never right.

predator—*n.* an animal that hunts another. A shark is a fierce <u>predator</u>, hunting other fish continuously, never sleeping, always hungry.

protein—*n.* a compound in all living things that helps organisms grow and repair themselves. Good sources of <u>protein</u> are beef and beans and eggs—which all happen to be in my favorite omelet!

proton—*n.* a positively charged particle in an atom. (See definitions of *electron* and *neutron*.)

protoplasm—*n.* a jellylike substance that forms all the living matter in plants and animals. That's right, the basis for all living things is a jiggly mass of jelly. Kind of gross when you think about it, so I try not to.

protozoa—*n.* primitive, single-celled organisms. <u>Protozoa</u> might be what the earliest forms of life on Earth were like.

pulley—*n.* a wheel with a groove in it that a rope fits on. By using <u>pulleys</u>, you can lift really, really heavy things. I went to a museum where a rope was attached to a 2,000-pound weight. It went through a series of <u>pulleys</u>, and they made it so you could lift 2,000 pounds with one hand. It was wild.

radiation—*n.* the emission of waves or particles. Nuclear <u>radiation</u> is waves and particles given off by radioactive material. It can be really dangerous and even lethal.

recessive trait—*n.* when paired with a dominant trait, it is the trait that "loses." (See the definition for *dominant trait*.)

renewable—*adj.* able to be used again. Most often used in the term "<u>renewable</u> resources" to describe sources of energy that can be used again and again. Two examples are wind and sunlight—they are forms of energy that you can use over and over without using up.

reproduction—*n.* the process by which living things produce offspring. Most animals and plants use sexual <u>reproduction</u>, where the offspring gets half its chromosomes from each parent. In asexual <u>reproduction</u>, the offspring gets all its genetic material from one parent. The formation of spores is a good example of asexual <u>reproduction</u>.

resistant—*adj.* able to fight off something. Some crops are engineered to be <u>resistant</u> to certain bugs. Some bacteria become resistant to drugs that are used to kill them. So <u>resistance</u> can be good for us (crops that can fend off pests) and bad for us (diseases that are <u>resistant</u> to treatment).

respiratory system—*n.* the group of organs that keep you breathing. If you think of it in terms of your house, things that circulate air—like fans and air conditioners—are your house's <u>respiratory</u> system. (See the Science exercise for all of the organs involved in your

Related Word

predatory—*adj.* like a hunter.

WhizFact

The Incredible Hulk was created when scientist Bruce Banner was accidentally exposed to radiation.

respiratory system.)

revolve—*v.* to move in a circular motion around a center. The Earth revolves around the sun. The Texas Rangers revolve around Alex Rodriguez. You get the picture.

rock cycle—*n.* a rock's life cycle, in which a rock goes from igneous to sedimentary to metamorphic by going through erosion, crushing, pressure, melting, and everything else rocks go through.

rotate—*n.* to turn on an axis. The Earth rotates on its axis. So do the other planets.

satellite—*n.* a man-made object shot into space that orbits the Earth or another planet. Most satellites these days are used for communication, but there are also science satellites and military satellites.

scientific method—*n.* the process of observing something, forming a hypothesis for how it works, doing experiments to test that hypothesis, and then drawing conclusions from your results. So, if from watching bears at the zoo, you form the hypothesis that bears are dumb as rocks, you do an experiment to test them. Maybe you ask them their names. When they don't know the answer, you conclude your hypothesis is correct—they don't know their names, they must be dumb as rocks. (You can see why the scientific method isn't perfect!)

sedimentary rock—*n.* rock that is formed near the Earth's surface by the accumulation of sediment. It's not metamorphic, it's not igneous—it's sedimentary! (See the definition for *rock cycle*.)

selective breeding—*n.* the process of choosing which plants or animals to breed with each other. You do this when you are looking to promote a particular trait. So if you are breeding poodles and you want poodles with extra long ears, you selectively breed the long-eared poodles. (You give the short-eared poodles away to friends.)

solar—*adj.* having to do with the sun. The solar system is the system of planets revolving around the sun. Solar flares are eruptions that spew from the sun and mess up our television reception. Solarcaine stops sunburn pain when someone you love is hurting.

soluble—*adj.* dissolvable. Sugar is soluble in water. So is Kool Aid.

stagnant—*adj.* motionless; not flowing. When water is stagnant, it becomes a prime breeding ground for mosquitoes. When the Texas Rangers offense is stagnant, that means they need to get some better hitters on the team.

stimulus—*n.* something that causes a response. An organism is always responding to both internal and external <u>stimuli</u>. For example, a toad responds to external <u>stimuli</u> like predators and temperature and internal <u>stimuli</u> like hunger and the urge to reproduce.

sustainable—*adj.* able to maintain over a period of time. One of the ways to fight world hunger is to find <u>sustainable</u> crops that starving countries can grow themselves. There is a Chinese proverb: "Give a man a fish and he will eat for a day. Teach a man to fish and he will eat for the rest of his life." That's the idea behind teaching people in these countries to grow <u>sustainable</u> crops.

synthesis—*n.* the combination of two or more things to make a brand new thing. I think the *Star Wars* movies are the perfect <u>synthesis</u> of special effects and a great story. Combining those two things has made a brand new thing—the best movie series ever.

tectonic plates—*n.* the huge plates that make up the continents and the floors of the oceans. They shift a little all of the time. The friction where the <u>tectonic plates</u> meet causes scary stuff to happen, including earthquakes, and mountains and tidal waves.

temperate—*adj.* not hot, not cold. This word is most often used when talking about <u>temperate</u> climates, where animals and plants thrive because the temperature does get too hot or cold.

toxic—*adj.* harmful; dangerous. Scientists deal with toxic materials all of the time. Sometimes we even work with them in science class ourselves. Stuff like mercury and dry ice are pretty cool, but they can be very <u>toxic</u>, so be careful.

trait—*n.* a characteristic; a feature. I share a lot of physical <u>traits</u> with my dad—we both have brown eyes, high foreheads, and winning smiles.

transform—*v.* to change from one thing into another. Coal <u>transforms</u> into diamonds under intense pressure after millions of years.

vacuum—*n.* a space where there is no matter. Lots of science experiments have to be done in a <u>vacuum</u> to work. For example, in a <u>vacuum</u>, a feather and a brick fall at the same rate, because there is no matter—air—to make the feather float more slowly.

vapor—*n.* stuff that looks like mist, fumes, or smoke. Steam is the <u>vapor</u> form of water.

velocity—*n.* speed. The highest <u>velocity</u> I have ever thrown my fastball is 72 mph.

water cycle—*n.* the cycle of evaporation and condensation that controls the distribution of water on Earth.

watershed—*n.* an area of high land where one side drains to one river system and the other side drains to another river system. Sherman, Texas, is on the <u>watershed</u> that splits the Red River and Trinity River.

watt—*n.* the fleshy orange fold of skin under a turkey's neck. Wait—that's a wattle! A <u>watt</u> is a unit of electricity. If you want to save electricity, change all the light bulbs in your house to 40-<u>watt</u> or 60-<u>watt</u> bulbs.

What kinds of sustainable crops are produced in your part of the state?

Think of Goldilocks: not too hot and not too cold, the "temperate soup" is just right!

Nature is full of transformations. Name three:
1.
2.
3.

71

WhizWords

acclimatization
conservation
ecosystem
fossil fuel
greenhouse effect
habitat
organism

Science

The Environment

Have you ever heard of Woody Guthrie? He was a folk singer who wrote hundreds of songs about America. He would travel the country hitchhiking and riding on freight trains, getting to know the people he met along the way. He ended up writing classics like "This Land Is Your Land," "Pastures of Plenty," and "Do-Re-Mi." (No, not the song about "a female deer" and "a drop of golden sun." A different "Do-Re-Mi.")

Guthrie was also a big environmentalist. He was really alarmed by all of the factories he saw going up around the country. He saw America as an expanse of forests and plains and deserts and lakes and rivers. And he saw it changing into an expanse of roads and cities and houses and, well, people.

My dad loves Woody Guthrie. He is always humming "This Land Is Your Land" and putting in his own words. So when he has to cut the grass he likes to sing, "This land is your land, this land is my land, I've got to cut the grass, that'll keep me smilin'." It can get annoying, but it gave me a great idea on how to remember environment words.

WRITE A FOLK SONG EXERCISE

What I want you to do is use each of these "Environment" words in a verse of "This Land Is Your Land." You want to squish the word and the definition into the verse. It may not win you any Grammys, but if you spend some time on it and fit all six words into six verses, you'll have a little hummable song about the environment. And you can hum it during a test if you need to remember the words!

I'll get you started with a verse about the WhizWord above—**fossil fuel**.

This land is your land,
this land is my land,
Fossil fuel emits carbon monoxide,
when you burn it in your car, man.

If you have another song you want to use instead of "This Land Is Your Land," by all means, go ahead. If you've never even heard "This Land Is Your Land," ask your music teacher to hum a few bars, or go on the Internet to *www.geocities.com/Nashville/3448/thisl1.html* to hear a snippet.

Science

The Body

By the end of middle school you should have a pretty good idea of what the different parts of the body do. The four main systems of the body aren't that hard to understand, but there are a lot of organs in each one, so it's good to be able to organize the organs by the systems they are in.

Just remember: the **circulatory system** has to do with circulating the blood. The **digestive system** has to do with organs that help you digest your food. The **respiratory system** does your breathing for you (to remember the word, think about being put on a respirator—a machine that breathes for you). And the **endocrine system**, well, it helps get the bad stuff out of your blood. Crime is bad—so think about the endo*crime* system getting the bad stuff out of your blood. Close enough!

LABELING YOUR INNARDS EXERCISE
I have listed the major organs in each system. Your challenge is to label them in this Britney Spears body outline. Check the answer key when you are done.

Circulatory System
arteries
capillaries
heart
lungs
veins

Science

Digestive System →
anus
esophagus
large intestine
mouth
small intestine
stomach

Respiratory System →
diaphragm
lungs
nose
pharynx (throat)
ribcage
trachea

The Body

Endocrine System →
adrenal glands
hypothalamus
ovaries (female)
pancreas
pituitary gland
testes (male)
thyroid gland

WhizWords

asteroids
eclipse
extraterrestrial
galaxy
light year
lunar
meteor
orbit
ozone layer
satellite
solar

Related Word

celestial—adj.
Asteroids and
satellites are
both **celestial**
bodies, as they
are part of the
universe.

Science
The Universe

Sometimes I just lie on my back in my backyard at night and look up at the sky and imagine what the astronauts on the International Space Station must think when they look out the window. Have you ever seen the movie *Apollo 13* or spent any time on NASA's website? The pictures of space from the windows of spacecraft are just incredible.

And now it looks like normal citizens are going to be able to go into space, just like the astronauts. In 2001, an American businessman named Dennis Tito became the first space tourist when he paid $20 million to join a Russian space crew on a trip to the International Space Station. So someday, you may get to travel in space, whether you're an astronaut or not.

DRAWING THE UNIVERSE EXERCISE

For this exercise you get to draw and label the universe, from the perspective of an astronaut on the old Mir. I have provided the Earth, its moon, and the sun. You can draw and/or label the rest of the "Universe" words above. For example:

LABEL OR DRAW
distance to sun in light years
a partial eclipse
the moon's orbit
the Earth's ozone layer
a satellite

WhizWords
cell
dominant trait
gene
genetics
recessive trait
trait

Science

Genetics

My friend Gene has curly red hair and freckles just like his father and all of his brothers. That's how I remember that a **gene** is the part of the **cell** that decides which **traits** will be passed from one generation to the next.

But sometimes **genetics** don't work out quite so logically. For instance, my sister Pam is really tall: 5'9". Both of my parents are short. So am I. So what happened to Pam? There must have been a **recessive** "tall" **gene** that both of my parents carried that, against the odds, made it into my sister. The same goes for her eye color. My parents both have brown eyes. I have brown eyes. My sister has blue eyes. So what happened to Pam? Again, a **recessive trait** in both my parents ended up being expressed in my freaky sister. Here's how that happens:

WhizTip
See *Innerspace!* It's a movie that came out in 1987 about a Navy pilot who gets minia-turized and injected into the body of a hypochondriac.

Bb			Bb
BB	Bb	Bb	bb
Brown	Brown	Brown	Blue

As you can see, three out of every four kids my parents would have would have brown eyes, because that is the **dominant gene** for eye color. All you need is one brown eyes **gene** to have brown eyes. Pam just got lucky and was the one kid who got a **recessive** "blue eyes" **gene** from each of my parents.

MOVIE AND TV STAR RECESSIVE TRAITS EXERCISE
Pick out two movie stars. I am going to pick Cher and Billy Crystal. Now, pick a trait. I am going to pick foot size and make big feet dominant and little feet recessive. Draw a chart like the one I drew above, giving each either two dominant genes (FF), two recessives (ff), or one of each (Ff). See how their children would turn out. Here is my Billy + Cher drawing.

I don't even want to think about what the rest of their bodies would look like.

Exercises

WhizWords

continental drift
erosion
fault
geology
mantle
tectonic plates

Science

Geology

WhizTip

Want to learn about Texas' geology? Start by going to The Texas Archaeological Society at www.txarch.org.

Living in Texas, you can forget that the world is a big mass of sliding **tectonic plates** drifting toward and away from each other, wreaking havoc where they butt up against each other. Everything here appears to be so flat and stable. But anyone who has studied the history of the Earth—and anyone who lives in California—knows that beneath us is a molten core of boiling rock, yearning to break free!

When you think of it this way, geology is pretty cool. In addition to studying the process of **continental drift**, geologists get to hunt for wild-looking fossils and try to piece them together like giant jigsaw puzzles. You can see why there are so many geologists running around, predicting earthquakes and digging up dinosaurs.

EARTHQUAKE EXERCISE

Unfortunately, geology is not always fun and games. Every once in a while a big earthquake hits and people lose their homes and sometimes their lives. The same forces that create mountains also create terrible tragedies.

For this exercise, I want you to research a recent earthquake. There was a massive earthquake in India in 2001 that killed tens of thousands. There was also an earthquake in San Francisco in 1989 that ruined the freeway system and ended up postponing a World Series game that was taking place when it hit!

Once you have compiled some information on an earthquake, turn the page. Write a short essay in the space provided using the words above to explain the tectonic shifts that caused the trembler. Underline the WhizWords in the essay.

Related Word

igneous rock
metamorphic rock
sedimentary rock

Essay

EXPLAIN THE TECTONIC SHIFTS BEHIND A RECENT EARTHQUAKE.

Chapter 5

Test Instructions

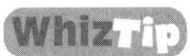

Use your pencil when you have reading passages on tests. Underline the topic sentence of each paragraph and circle proper names. It will help slow you down and help you when you refer back to the passage for information.

Circle your answer to the following best questions: Which word best describes George W. Bush?

man woman child

What is your best prediction of how the Texas Rangers will do this year?

better worse same

Which word best answers the question "Where is Austin?"
Earth
Texas
Not in Minnesota

according to the passage—When you see this phrase, you know the answer to the question is right in the passage you just read. You don't have to use your imagination or remember what you learned in class to find an answer. The answer to the question is in the reading passage.

accurate—*adj.* exactly right. As in "Which of the following is an accurate statement?" This means "Which statement matches the information given?" For example, if the information says Pam spit out her broccoli when her mom wasn't looking because broccoli makes her sick, an accurate statement would be "Pam can't stand broccoli," not "Pam can't stand her mother."

approximate—*v.* to come close to; to estimate. Sometimes tests ask you to approximate—that means you are supposed to use the information they give you to make an estimate. Estimates are answers that are close to the real answer. When you are in a car accident, the repair shop gives an estimate on how much the repairs will cost. This is approximately how much it will cost. It may be a little more, it may be a little less.

author's purpose—the writer's reason for writing, as in "the author's purpose in this passage is to. . . . " In author's purpose questions, you are looking for what the author was trying to accomplish with his writing. Sometimes an author's purpose is to scare you (horror novel). Sometimes an author's purpose is to convince you to believe something (persuasive article). Think about how you felt after reading the passage—how you felt is probably the author's purpose.

best—*adj.* you'll see this word a lot: "best represents;" "best estimate;" "best prediction;" "best describes;" "the best summary;" "best supported by information in the passage." It means you have to use your "best judgment" and pick the "best answer." You may have a set of answers that may all seem like they could be right, and you have to choose the one that is the best (more right than the others).

complete the pattern—also seen on tests as "if the pattern continues . . . . " This phrase is used on number pattern questions.

WhizList

The test is asking you to find the next number in a number pattern. Figure out what the pattern is, and fill in the next—or missing—number to <u>complete the pattern</u>.

conclude—*v.* to form an opinion based on information. As in "the reader can <u>conclude</u> . . . . " That just means, "What did the reader (you) think after reading this passage?"

convince—*v.* to persuade. As in "information to <u>convince</u> the reader . . . . " Some tests ask you if an author provided enough examples to convince you of something. So if I wanted to <u>convince</u> you the Texas Rangers are going to win the World Series this year, I'd have to provide a ton of reasons to persuade you.

corresponds—*v.* matches; agrees with. Sometimes you are asked to pick the answer that <u>corresponds</u> to the data in the question. That just means it matches. So a test may have a statement like:

The *Star Wars* trilogy became the highest grossing movie series ever, earning more than $1 billion.

And then it says:

Pick the statement that <u>corresponds</u> to the data given in the statement:

A) The *Star Wars* trilogy lost money.

B) The *Star Wars* trilogy won three Oscars.

C) The *Star Wars* trilogy made a lot of money.

equivalent—*adj.* the same as. Test questions—especially math and science test questions—often want you to find things that are <u>equivalent</u> to one another. That just means finding an answer that is the same as something in the question. So if a test wants you to find the <u>equivalent</u> to a dozen eggs, you pick 12 eggs. If a test wants you to find the <u>equivalent</u> of 1/2 meter, you pick 50 centimeters.

expression—*n.* a way of saying something, usually with a math equation. As in "which <u>expression</u> could be used . . . . " or "which <u>expression</u> represents . . . . " So you are trying to match the <u>expression</u> to the passage. A passage may say:

Tim bought five eggs, dropped three, and then purchased five more.

Related Word

The word **corresponds is related to the words accurate, equivalent, and exactly.**

Which <u>expression</u> represents Tim's egg-buying experience?

A) 5 + 3 + 5

B) 5 − 3 − 5

C) 5 − 3 + 5

fact—*n.* something that ACTUALLY happened or ACTUALLY exists. As in "Which of these is a FACT in this passage?" For some reason, the TAAS CAPITALIZES this word when it is used in a question. And when there is a question about FACT, there is usually a question about OPINION, too. A FACT is what actually happened. An OPINION is what someone thinks.

main idea—as in "The main idea of the story." You get a <u>main idea</u> by reading a passage carefully. Sometimes the title of a reading passage offers a clue about the <u>main idea</u>. Sometimes it's better to decide the passage's <u>main idea</u> *before* you read the answer choices. You will usually find your <u>main idea</u> among the answer choices. But if you read the answer choices first, it can get confusing, because usually all the ideas in the answer choices are in the passage, but they aren't the <u>main idea</u>.

method—*n.* one way of doing things. As in "Which method could be used to . . . . " Sometimes math problems ask you which <u>method</u> can be used to get the right answer. This just means "Which of the answer choices is a way you can get the right answer." One way to find out is to do the math problem, and then pick the <u>method</u> you used to get the answer.

most likely—as in "which is most likely to be true . . . . " This means the answer is what is probably going to happen. At least there is a better chance it will happen than the other answers. The answer to a "<u>most likely</u>" question usually isn't spelled out in the reading passage. You have to guess what is <u>most likely</u> to happen, based on the information in the passage.

not here—this is the TAAS's version of "none of the above." It just means the right answer is not listed, so you pick "not here."

opinion—*n.* something someone believes or thinks, whether it is true or not. As in "Which is an OPINION in this passage?" Being able to tell the difference between FACTS and OPINIONS is important for the reading sections of the TAAS. (See the definition of FACT for more on this.)

probably—*adv.* most likely. Another popular word on the TAAS! Most often used as "<u>probably</u> felt . . . " or "<u>probably</u> believes . . . " or "<u>probably</u> thought . . . . " It just means that the passage doesn't actually state what a character or writer believes, but from reading it, you should be able to tell anyway.

reasonable—*adj.* logical; showing good judgment. <u>Reasonable</u> is like "best." You'll see it all the time: "Which is a <u>reasonable</u> total cost . . . " or "what is a <u>reasonable</u> prediction . . . " or "what is a

reasonable conclusion . ... " or "what is a <u>reasonable</u> length . . . . "
Who is the most <u>reasonable</u> person you know? The most <u>reasonable</u> person I can think of is the newsman Tom Brokaw. You know who I'm talking about—he reads the nightly news for one of the networks. He seems very <u>reasonable</u>—like I can trust him. Whenever I get a "reasonable" question, I think—which answer would Mr. <u>Reasonable</u>, Tom Brokaw, choose? You can do the same thing. Just pick out the most <u>reasonable</u> person you know and try to choose the answer you think he would choose.

reason to believe—as in "gives the reader reason to believe . . . ." This means the passage makes you think one way, not the other way. For example, here's a sample passage: "The Dallas Cowboys have drafted the 10 best players in college football, and the other teams in the NFL weren't allowed to draft anyone at all." This passage gives you <u>reason to believe</u> that:

    a) The Cowboys will get better.

    b) The other teams in the NFL will get better.

The answer is (a). You have <u>reason to believe</u> that if the Cowboys got all the good players and the other teams didn't get any players at all, the Cowboys will get better, not the other teams, even though it doesn't actually say that in the passage.

rounded to the nearest—as in " . . . <u>rounded to the nearest</u> thousand." When a test question asks you to round off, that means you go to the place given (tens, hundreds, thousands) and round up or down. If the next number is five or higher, you round up one. If the next number is four or lower, you round down one. On "<u>rounded to the nearest</u>" questions, it's very important to pay attention to whether the question is asking you to round to tens, hundreds, thousands, or whatever.

suggests—*v.* leads you to believe. As in "the information in the passage <u>suggests</u> . . . . " This just means the information doesn't come right out and say something, it just hints at it. It's kind of like a "probably" question—you have to read the passage carefully and trust your understanding of it.

WhizWords

according to the passage
author's purpose
main idea

Test Instructions

Reading Carefully

Related Word

conclude—v. to
reach an answer.
Tests are always
asking you
what you can
conclude from a
reading passage.

As you know by now, being able to read things and understand what you read is very important to doing well on the TAAS and other tests. The way tests figure out how well you are understanding things is by using these three "Reading Carefully" phrases. So it helps if you get used to answering questions that use these words, no matter what kind of reading it is.

My favorite things to read are, in order, the online *Dallas Morning News* sports page, *Sports Illustrated,* and the Harry Potter series. So as long as J. K. Rowling keeps pumping out books, the Rangers keep playing baseball, and NASCAR keeps going strong, I am going to be reading for the rest of my life. You probably have some favorite reading materials, too. That's what we are going to use in this next exercise.

READING WHAT YOU LIKE EXERCISE
Open your favorite book, magazine, or newspaper, or go to your favorite website. Pick a passage or article that's about one to three pages long. If you use a website, print out the article. Read it carefully, using your pencil to circle important names and underline important sentences. Take your time, really "get into" the writing. When you are done reading, write three sentences that start with these words:

> The author's purpose in this article is . . . .
> According to this passage, the author thinks . . . .
> The main idea of this passage is . . . .

Do this with at least five different kinds of writing. If you like doing it, do it a lot. It takes, like, five extra minutes, and you'll end up remembering a ton more stuff about things you actually like.

Test Instructions
Probably

Not everything in life is absolutely, positively 100 percent obviously true. Come to think of it, almost nothing is. That means you have to get used to recognizing degrees of possibility.

For example, the Texas Rangers are **probably** going to be really good for a long time because they have the best shortstop in baseball, Alex Rodriguez. And it's **reasonable** to **suggest** that Britney Spears is going to be popular for a long time because she's so . . . talented.

What's my point? My point is that even if you don't know something is absolutely, positively 100 percent obviously true, you can still **probably** know a whole bunch of things. And on tests, one of the keys to doing well is being able to figure out what is **reasonable**, and what is not.

If you are having trouble on tests figuring out what is **probably** true, a good way to get some perspective on things is to think "What would Mr. **Reasonable** do?" And everyone knows who the most **reasonable** people on the planet are. Newscasters!

Related Word

approximate—v. to come close to; to estimate. Math tests often ask you to approximate something, which means using the information they give you to get an answer in a general range.

MR. REASONABLE EXERCISE

If you don't watch the nightly news already, take a half an hour out of your busy schedule for a few nights and watch the Big Three: CBS (Dan Rather), NBC (Tom Brokaw), and ABC (Peter Jennings). Pick the newscaster who strikes you as the most reasonable of the bunch—the guy who would probably pick the right answer on a test. Mine is Tom Brokaw. He seems like he would make a good, reasonable guess.

Now get a pencil and paper. Write your guy's name on the top of a piece of paper. Now sit down with a parent or friend and watch the news! Have your news buddy write down four questions about news stories from the nightly news, using the four "Probably" words. For example:

Is it reasonable to suggest that Iraqi President Saddam Hussein will make nice with President George W. Bush?

Before you answer, think "How would Tom Brokaw answer?" Do this every night for a week, and you'll probably get the hang of the "Probably" words and questions.

Hint: One way to be sure you've come up with the right answer to a question using a "Probably" word is to write a response that includes the word "because," *because* this will require you to go back to the reading passage to find information to prove your point. If you can't find evidence to back up your answer, you're *probably* wrong.

Chapter 6
All-Purpose Words

List the three classmates you collaborate with the most:
1. _____
2. _____
3. _____

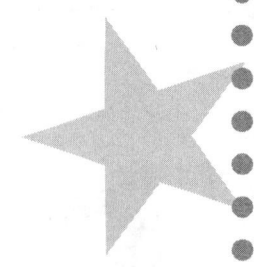

Antonym

inconvenient—adj. a lot of trouble.

collaborate—*v.* to work together. You learn best when you <u>collaborate</u> in the classroom. My science teacher has us <u>collaborate</u> on projects, but I've been having trouble getting anyone to work with me since I accidentally lit my lab partner's notebook on fire with a Bunsen burner.

consistent—*adj.* steady; always the same. The best way to do well on tests is to be <u>consistent</u> with your studying. Cramming for tests may work once in a while, but in the end you won't remember as much.

constructive—*adj.* helpful. The word is most commonly used in the phrase "<u>constructive</u> criticism," which means you are doing something wrong, but the person telling you is only trying to help by pointing out your errors and showing you how to improve.

contradiction—*n.* something that disagrees with something else. You have probably heard the phrase "a <u>contradiction</u> in terms." That's when two words in a row <u>contradict</u> each other, like: "an easy test." Tests aren't usually easy. Tests also often ask you to find <u>contradictions</u> in stories and passages. That is where two statements or pieces of information do not agree with each other.

convenient—*adj.* easy; handy. This book is incredibly <u>convenient</u> to keep around. It's small, and it has tons of the words you need to know. Just put it in your bookbag and keep it there. Whenever you have a question about a word, this book will be <u>conveniently</u> in your bag and you can look it up.

conventional—*adj.* normal; accepted. One phrase that's used a lot is "<u>conventional</u> wisdom," as in: <u>Conventional</u> wisdom says that short people aren't that successful at basketball.

logical—*adj.* reasonable; making sense. <u>Logical</u> is kind of the opposite of *emotional*. When you get emotional on tests, you can really mess up. Try to stay <u>logical</u> as much as you can, going from one question to the next without getting too up or too down.

objective—*adj.* fair; impartial. To remember this word, just think about what kind of opinions an "object" like a chair would have. Answer: no opinions, objects don't have opinions.

precise—*adj.* exact; accurate. Tests kind of go back and forth from asking you to be <u>precise</u> with your answers to asking you to figure out what something means in general. So make sure you pay attention to <u>precisely</u> what the test question asks for.

predict—*v.* to guess in advance. Some test questions ask you to <u>predict</u> what will happen in an experiment or in a story. That means you are supposed to look at the facts and make a logical conclusion as to what will happen. (See definitions of *logical* in this chapter and *conclusion* in English Language Arts chapter.)

relevant—*adj.* related to the matter at hand. Sometimes on tests, you are asked to use only <u>relevant</u> information—that means information that matters (as opposed to stuff that does not matter). For example, if you are taking a test on making cheese, milk is <u>relevant</u>, because it's an ingredient in cheese, while information on fingernails is not <u>relevant</u> (it is <u>irrelevant</u>).

strategic—*adj.* planned. This word is used a lot when talking about war—especially about generals' "<u>strategic</u> maneuvers." Chess is a game that also requires a lot of "<u>strategic</u> maneuvers." Speaking of which, when you are taking tests, it can be important for you to have a <u>strategy</u> going in, like "I am going to stay cool no matter what" or "I am going to do the easy questions first and the hard ones second." Both of those are good <u>strategies</u>.

systematic—*adj.* acting according to an organized plan. <u>Systematic</u> is a lot like *strategic*—they both are used a lot when talking about a powerful person, like a general or dictator, who has a master plan and a strategy and a system to carry it out.

tangible—*adj.* touchable; real. This book is <u>tangible</u>—it is real and you can touch it. The word is used a lot in the phrase "<u>tangible</u> benefits," which means good things that actually happen. For example, my friend Kevin realized the <u>tangible</u> benefits of all his time in the kitchen when he won first prize in the cake baking contest.

Try to predict your grade on a test before you take it, then see how close you are to your prediction.

irrelevant—adj. not pertaining to the matter at hand.

intangible—adj. not touchable.

WhizWords

All of 'em.

All-Purpose Words
Celebrity Hot Tub

WhizTip

You can also do this with flash cards—write the word on one side, and the question using the word's definition on the other.

Did you ever want to be one of those reporters on *Entertainment Tonight* or *Extra* or *Inside Edition* that just spends all of his or her time running around, interviewing celebrities at parties? Or better yet, a VJ on MTV who just hangs out and chats with bands and singers who come by the show's studios? Well, I have.

My idea is that I'd have the celebrities over to my house and interview them sitting in my parents' hot tub. We'd relax in our bathing suits, sip lemonade, and talk about whatever they wanted to talk about. I'm actually thinking about doing this for my public access cable station or doing a webcast. I just haven't figured out how to arrange the microphones without all of us getting electrocuted.

CELEBRITY HOT TUB EXERCISE
For this exercise you are going to need a pad and pencil. Write down "Celebrity Hot Tub" at the top of a page. Now, go to one of the chapters and write down ten words that you are having trouble with. Just read through the words and definitions from one chapter and pick out ten words where you are still a little shaky, Here are ten I picked from social studies:

compensation	pragmatist
deter	qualifications
eligible	resolute
impose	subversive
insurgent	usurp

Now form a question that you would ask a celebrity who joined you for Celebrity Hot Tub. Use the definition as part of your question. For example, this is a question that I would ask supermodel/actress James King.

Q: Ms. King, are you a pragmatist about your acting career? By that I mean, are you realistic about the roles you are going to get?

After you have written questions using ten words from one chapter, go ahead and write questions with words from the other chapters, too. Keep these all in one place so you can go back and review them (or ask them, should you ever find James King sharing your hot tub).

All-Purpose Words

Word of the Day

You know those daily calendars that look like a block of Post-it Notes? You peel off a page every day and learn something new—every day. My favorite one is the *Far Side* cartoon-of-the-day calendar. I even have a bunch of my favorite *Far Side* calendar pages taped to the inside of my locker. My favorite one is "The Night of the Crash Test Dummies"—it has all these crash test dummies attacking some poor guy in his car.

Anyway, the cool thing about that calendar and all the others is that you get to see something new every day. And that's the best way to learn vocabulary words, by using them every day.

Related Word

consecutive—adj. occuring in order, one right after the other. For this exercise, you are going to be learning words consecutively, one right after the other.

VOCABULARY CALENDAR EXERCISE

Until I can convince my book's publisher to make a WordWhiz word-a-day calendar, you are going to have to make one for yourself! This exercise will take an afternoon, so wait until you have a few hours to kill—maybe when it's raining out or you are home sick from school—to get started.

You can make this calendar one of two ways:

> With a brick of Post-It Notes
> With some other "something-a-day" calendar

If you use Post-Its, first go through them and make them into a calendar, writing down the days and months left in this year. (Use a wall calendar to find the correct days.)

If you use another calendar, find one that has a lot of empty space where you can write down a word and its definition.

Now, there are about 600 words in this book. You need to choose the 365 words (or however many days are left on your calendar) that you need to learn the most. Now write the word and its definition on your calendar.

When you are done, put your calendar somewhere you will see it the first thing in the morning: by your bed, on the sink in the bathroom—wherever. Read the word-a-day aloud, repeat it and its definition three times, then put it in your pocket. Try to use that word as much as you can on its day.

Word Whiz

Texas Middle School

Answer Pages

Here are my answers to the Whiz Quizzes and Exercises.
To find out how you did on quizzes and exercises that ask you
to write essays, create calendars, and otherwise use
your creativity, run your answer past an adult who can decide whether
or not you have used the vocabulary words correctly.

English Language Arts

Whiz Quizzes

page 8
Use an adjective or adverb to
describe each of these words:

The pizza at lunch today was
unbelievably chewy. It was like
eating pizza-flavored gum.

My soccer team has *bright*
green uniforms.

I go to a *small* school.

My mom had a *fabulous* shopping
experience last week—she got four
pairs of shoes for the price of one.

I play a lot of *physical* sports, like
soccer and football.

Difficult questions on tests make me
concentrate even harder.

page 10
Turn the following into their
contractions:
is + not = isn't
we + are = we're

were + not = weren't
she + is = she's

page 11
List three euphemisms you or
your parents use:

If I don't get *Tomb Raider*
I'm going to lose it.

Grandpa Antonio is a few cards
short of a full deck.

If the Rangers lose again
I'm going to be ill.

page 12
Identify the part of speech of
the following words:

blonde—adj., n.
threaten—v.
fake—adj., n., v.
mambo—n., v.

Note: As you probably can tell by now,
many words have meanings that have
multiple parts of speech.

page 13
Write the following sentences using metaphors:

Pam is <u>greased lightning</u>.

James is <u>two French fries short of a Happy Meal</u>.

Fabio <u>vacuums up ice cream</u> like there is no tomorrow.

page 14
Write down your favorite (or least favorite) platitude:

Least favorite: Life is a bowl of cherries.

Write down the premise of the last movie you saw:

There's Something About Mary
Everyone was in love with a girl named Mary, but only one geeky guy was her soulmate.

page 15
Write a one-sentence summary of the last book you read:

The Old Man and the Sea
An old man hadn't caught any fish in quite some time, then he caught the biggest fish anyone had ever seen and had to bring it in to shore all by himself.

Social Studies

Whiz Quizzes
page 20
Name three rules at school that you advocate:

1. Raising your hand before answering a question.

2. Maintaining a 3.0 GPA gets you in unsupervised study hall.

3. No shirt, no shoes, no service.

page 21
Write down your three most arduous classes in school:

Math
Science
Social Studies

page 27
Write an epigram about learning vocabulary words:

A vocabulary word learned is a vocabulary word earned.

page 28
List three things you once thought were futile:

1. Getting Alex Rodriguez to play for the Texas Rangers.

2. Reaching a height of 5 feet tall.

3. Achieving the high score on *Arctic Thunder*.

Write down a hardship you have gone through:

I recently broke my wrist and had to sit out half a season of baseball.

page 29
Who was the first president to be impeached?

President Andrew Johnson

page 33
Name your nemesis!

The big bopper on our team's arch rivals the Buford Bears. I don't know his name, but he keeps hitting home runs off of me.

Name your favorite team's main opposition:

The New York Yankees

Answer Pages

page 39
Name a limitation you have
had to transcend in your life:

I was really impatient a few years ago and
got upset over unimportant things. I have
worked hard to be more patient and mellow.

Exercises
page 41
Government

Country	Year	Government
England	1714	Monarchy
Texas	1836	Republic
United States	1897	Democracy
Germany	1935	Fascism
Jordan	1953	Monarchy
Cambodia	1976	Despotism
England	1979	Democracy

Math

Whiz Quizzes
page 46
Pick the next number in
these number patterns:
3, 6, 9, 12, <u>15</u>
−3, −1, 1, 3, <u>5</u>
3/4, 1 1/2, 2 1/4, <u>3</u>

page 48
Circle the integers.
1/2
.6
6
−6
−2
0
3.2
6.9
3/4
17
−12
243

page 51
Please square these numbers:
$2^2 = 4$
$45^2 = 2025$
$-3^2 = 9$
$-41^2 = 1681$
$7^2 = 49$
$-6^2 = 36$

page 52
Solve the following problems with the
variables $x=2$ and $y=3$:

$2x = 2(2) = 4$
$4y = 4(3) = 12$
$-5y = -5(3) = -15$
$x - y = 2 - 3 = -1$
$2y + 7x = 2(3) + 7(2) = 6 + 14 = 20$
$-2x - 4y = -2(2) - 4(3) = -4 - 12 = -16$

Exercises
Circles
page 55

Quarter	d= 2(1 in) = 2 in
	c= 2π(1in) = 2π in
CD	d= 2(7cm) = 14 cm
	c= 2π(7cm) = 14π cm
Tire	d= 2(12 in) = 24 in
	c= 2π(12 in) = 24π in

Number Types
page 56
$.79
positive number, rational number

.327
positive number, rational number

2 1/2
positive number, rational number

4
integer, positive number,
rational number, whole number

-12
integer, negative number,
rational number, whole number

6π
irrational number, positive number

Number Relationships
page 57

	Mean	Median	Mode
English	85.71	92	92
Math	85.43	82	78
Science	94.43	94	94
Social Studies	83.86	84	84
O'Neill	.291	.285	.256
Ramirez	.313	.309	none
Rodriguez	.300	.305	none
Jeter	.323	.324	none
Gwynn	.336	.329	.317

Science

Whiz Quizzes
page 62
Name five organisms that are part of an ecosystem at or near your home.

1. Koi fish
2. cat
3. front lawn
4. evergreen trees
5. ants

page 63
Name three more extinct animals or species.

1. Dodo bird
2. Tasmanian tiger wolf
3. Sea cow

page 64
Think of a name for your generation that is better than Generation I.

My pick: Generation Perfect

page 65
Identify the rock's type:

Basalt—igneous
Granite—igneous
Limestone—sedimentary
Marble—metamorphic

What's another kind of insulation?

My sleeping bag insulates me from the cold when I camp out..

Which is longer?

100 feet of string
2,000 miles of highway
350-meter running track
Small intestine

page 66
List three things that are lethal to humans:

1. Some kinds of cancer
2. Power lines
3. Extreme hot or cold

page 67
Name a genetic mutation that helped this species survive:

Giraffe—long neck
Human—opposable thumbs
Elephant—big tusks
Cheetah—extreme speed

page 68
What is your town of origin?

San Antonio

page 71
What kinds of sustainable crops are produced in your part of the state?

Corn and soybeans.

Nature is full of transformations. Name three:

1. Caterpillars transform into butterflies.
2. Ice transforms into water (and vice versa).
3. Seeds transform into flowers.

Test Instructions

Whiz Quizzes

page 80

Circle your answers to the following "best" questions:

Man
Better
Texas

page 82

Circle the facts and underline the opinions.

The Rangers hit 173 home runs in 2000.

They are going to do better this year.

The Yankees beat the Rangers when they met in the playoffs in 1998.

The Rangers will beat the Yankees the next time they meet.

Alex Rodriguez is the best shortstop ever.

All-Purpose Words

Whiz Quizzes

page 86

List the three classmates you collaborate with most:

Frank
Judy
Mookie

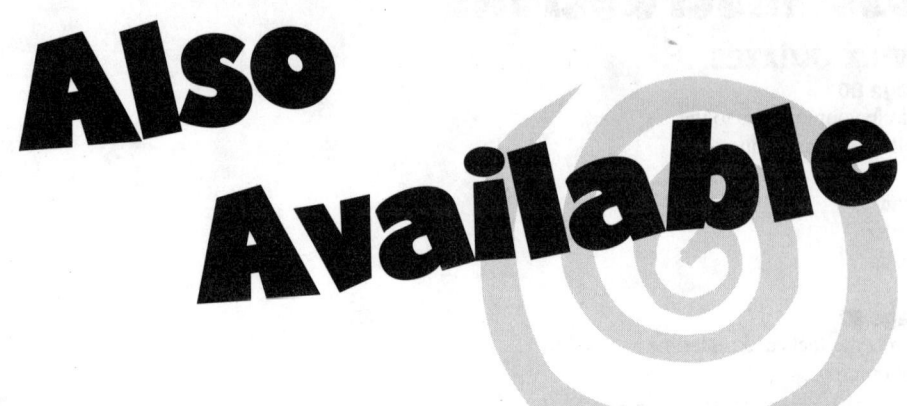

Also Available

20-Minute Learning Connection:
Texas Middle School Edition

Crusade in the Classroom:
How George W. Bush's Education Reforms Will Affect Your Children, Our Schools

Ultimate TAAS: Expert Tips to Help Boost Your Grade 8 Score